# Getting Better,
# Not Bitter

# Getting Better, Not Bitter

A Spiritual Prescription
for Breast Cancer

Brenda Ladun

New Hope Publishers

Birmingham, Alabama

New Hope Publishers
P. O. Box 12065
Birmingham, AL 35202-2065
www.newhopepubl.com

Library of Congress Cataloging-in-Publication Data
Ladun, Brenda, 1962–
    Getting better, not bitter : a spiritual prescription for breast
cancer / Brenda Ladun.
        p. cm.
    ISBN 1-56309-733-8 (pbk.)
    1. Ladun, Brenda, 1962–    . 2. Breast cancer—Patients
—Religious life.  3. Breast cancer—Religious aspects—Christian-
ity.    I. Title.
BV4910.33.L33 2002
248.8'619699449--dc21

                                                    2002008210

Unless otherwise noted, all Scripture references are taken from the HOLY BIBLE, NEW INTERNATIONAL VERSION®. NIV®. Copyright©1973, 1978, 1984 by International Bible Society. Used by permission of Zondervan. All rights reserved.

Scripture references marked (TEV) are taken from the Good News Bible in Today's English Version—Second Edition, Copyright© 1992 by American Bible Society. Used by permission.

Scripture references marked (TLB) are taken from *The Living Bible*, copyright© 1971. Used by permission of Tyndale House Publishers, Inc., Wheaton, IL 60189 USA. All rights reserved.

Cover design by Righteous Planet
Back cover photo by Karim Shamsi-Basha

ISBN: 1-56309-733-8
N024122 • 0902 • 12M1

# Dedication

To my husband Doug—
Thanks for sticking by me
during the storms of life.

And to my children,
who had to grow up a little faster
because of my breast cancer—
Thanks for being so sweet and careful
with me while I was fragile,
and for being my inspiration
to get strong again
spiritually, mentally, and physically.

# Table of Contents

*Getting Better, Not Bitter*

# *Introduction*

*A* breast cancer diagnosis can be devastating. For some, it's hard even to accept what's happened to you. I know I had to pray about it—a lot. I felt as if I was being pounded, blow after blow after blow. Hit with the diagnosis, hit again after the surgery, hit again by chemo, hit again and again.

I think of this book as a conversation with a sister or brother. That's one of the many things that cancer did for me. It made me realize how a community really can be like a family. In this book I share some very personal moments from the first year of my battle with breast cancer. But it's that kind of information that can help you—before or after surgery—to deal with the shock and emotional pain that often comes with a cancer diagnosis. Before cancer, I would blush if I had to talk about my body. But now I realize this information must be shared to empower other cancer patients.

I hope you gain strength from the story of my cancer battle. I share my tears, my laughter, and most of all, my faith. I hope you'll chuckle at some of the bizarre things that have happened in the past year. I show you the highlights and the shadows during that time. I believe the more we talk about cancer and work to fight it together, the closer we come to a cure.

But most of all, I hope to share my faith and how God wrapped His arms around me and my family and held us during the heat of the battle. I'll tell you how God molded me and took something very bad and produced many blessings. I feel I'm better physically, mentally, and spiritually as a result of having cancer. How did I go from being so weak that I couldn't go to the bathroom alone to running the first marathon of my life? You'll find the answers in this book.

# Chapter One

# News Anchor, But Really Just Another Mom!

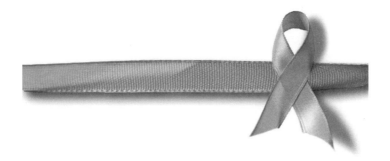

$\mathcal{M}$y mother still chuckles about the fact that, other than mama and dada, my first word was *busy*. I'd watch Mom flutter around the house cleaning, and she'd say *busy, busy, busy*, and I repeated it. I never really walked; I crawled, then I ran. She thinks it's funny that I've been busy ever since.

Why can't I be one of those sit-by-the-sea-and-ponder people? I guess because God has a plan for each one of us. For me, He must have said, "This one will be busy." But aren't all moms busy? Moms know, from the time they get up in the morning until the time they drop into bed after cleaning up and giving goodnight kisses, it's a day packed full. Many women balance a career with their responsibilities at home, as I do.

I'm a news anchor, and five days a week I anchor the six and ten o'clock news. I also spend my days at work developing and producing stories for those newscasts. No two days are exactly the same in this job. Chaos can take over at any moment because of breaking news. We have to be ready to respond at a moment's notice to deliver the story. For instance, when a truck carrying dangerous chemicals crashes on the interstate, I warn drivers to steer clear of the dangerous area. It's a job I always take pride in, knowing the information we deliver makes a difference in many lives.

What's a typical day like in the life of a news anchor? My workday starts when most other people's day winds down. I go to work at 2:00 pm, and the day begins with a strategy meeting. Anchors, reporters, producers, photographers, and the news director meet to talk about the important stories of the day. The producer decides what will be in the newscast. During the afternoon, I might shoot or write a story that will air that evening.

While I enjoy anchoring, reporting is what makes my job fun. I think staying connected to the community is important. I like talking to people. Helping resolve an elderly woman's phone bill problem or talking to a 76-year-old marathon runner is a kick for me.

## Cancer Opened My Eyes

But most importantly, I'm a mom. God has trusted me to take care of a husband and three little boys—and a dog named Copper. I know that viewers may forget last night's news story in years to come, but the values I teach my children will live on for generations. As a mom I have an awesome job, but sometimes I get too busy to enjoy this gift.

Cancer helped open my eyes to the fact that every day is a gift from God, one that we can open and enjoy just as we would a Christmas present. Before cancer, I didn't see the big picture; I only saw the busy work, much like Martha of Bethany. The Bible story found in Luke 10:38–42 describes how Jesus came to Martha's town, and she welcomed Him. Her sister Mary sat at Jesus' feet listening to Him, but Martha was busy, busy, busy. She was doing everything she *should* do, and it kept her running all the time. She worked hard to prepare a meal for Jesus and to show Him he was welcome in her home. Martha got angry with her sister Mary because she was not helping with the busy work.

> *"Martha, Martha,' the Lord answered, 'you are worried and upset about many things, but only one thing is needed. Mary has chosen what is better, and it will not be taken away from her.'"* —Luke 10:41–42

Jesus urged her to remember that "only one thing is needed." Keep the story of Martha in mind while I describe a much-too-busy existence.

## Typical Mom Day

It started out as one of those mornings. You could almost hear the cartoon hurry-music in the background. I got up, got breakfast ready, made sure I hadn't forgotten to make a lunch or check off the school to-do list. Sweet 3-year-old Gabby needed a shoebox to make an Easter basket at school, and 6-year-old Brooks had to remember show and tell. Oops, I almost forgot to include the permission slip for the field trip to the cookie factory.

My 6-month-old baby boy, Garrett, with his big blue eyes and blond peach fuzz, couldn't seem to shake that cold. I called our pediatrician, Dr. Lisa

Conry, who over the years has become a friend. "Hello, yes, nothing serious. Garrett has had the sniffles for more than a week now. Okay, I'll bring him in just to make sure." With the third child, I didn't rush to the doctor at the first sign of a sniffle, but there was something about that cold I didn't like.

"Alright guys, stop fighting over the last sausage; you'll have to split it. We have ten minutes to get out the door. Time to brush your teeth." While I barked orders like a drill sergeant, I poured what had become my morning inspiration on 4 hours of sleep. Coffee...it's a vice, but a much-needed one, considering the week I'd had. I had tried to do without the stuff, but literally fell asleep at a red light once after dropping off the boys at school.

Why didn't I sleep? Well, once I got home from work at 11:00, there were dishes to do, things to pick up, and projects to catch up on. Then finally, after jumping into my jammies and feeling like I might be lucky enough to get to sleep... "whaaaaaa!" It was baby Garrett. That cold was making him fussy and he couldn't sleep. So at midnight it was time to rock-a-bye baby. Even though I was dead tired, it was a precious quiet moment with this little one. After an hour we both nodded off. I'm not sure who was drooling more, Garrett or

Mom. I woke up and wiped the drool from both our mouths. "Okay little guy, back in the crib you go," I said.

Then Garrett responded, "whaaaaa!" Before I could finally get him settled, it was 3:00 am. The boys get us up at 6:30—I still got three and a half hours of sleep. Something is better than nothing!

## A Baby Scare

The next morning at the pediatrician, we were waiting in the exam room. I was playing with my little bald-headed, blue-eyed baby. He got so excited, he started kicking and thrashing and giggling while he was on the exam table. He was breathing a little heavy, but it was almost as if he were running in place. When the doctor walked in, she listened to him breathe...then listened again...and again. That's when I began to worry.

"He's breathing a little fast," she said. "I'd like to give him a breathing treatment and see what happens." My heart sank. My sweet, beautiful little baby had something wrong? I didn't even think the fast breathing was a problem. He wasn't gasping for air, just breathing a little fast.

The doctor left the room, and a few minutes later a nurse brought a strange-looking machine into the room. "Here's how you do it," she said. She covered his nose with a cone-shaped piece of plastic attached to the machine. She poured a drug into a receptacle connected to the device. She said, "I'll be back." Then she left me on my own to cover my baby's nose and mouth with this contraption. Awkwardly, I cradled little Garrett in my arms and pushed the nozzle to his nose. At first he looked at me as if to ask, *What's happening, Mom?* Then he screamed at the top of his lungs. That's when I felt weak. As my baby's tears rolled down his little face, my tears started rolling, too. I couldn't imagine what must have been going through his mind.

The doctor came back into the room, gently took the device off Garrett's face, and listened to his breathing. Then again, and again. "The treatment slowed his breathing down," she said. "While that's good, it shows that he needs the treatment. This could be a virus or possibly the beginning of asthma. Let's do the treatments three times a day for a month. Then we'll see what happens."

The machine arrived at our home, and by the end of a month, Garrett's breathing seemed to be under control. After a few months of checkups, baby Garrett's breathing seemed normal. He was okay, but my nerves had taken a beating. With the latest report of good health, though, the trouble hopefully was behind us.

## Little Did I Know

Life continued at its normal chaotic pace. Like Martha in Luke 10, I found little time to thank God for each beautiful day, to listen to the birds sing in the morning, and to receive the gifts God had for me each day.

Little did I know that while I was battling my baby's health problem, I had a sneaky, deadly disease growing silently in my body—and I felt fine. It was a cancer that would change how I looked at everything in my life.

# Chapter Two

# The Perfect Life

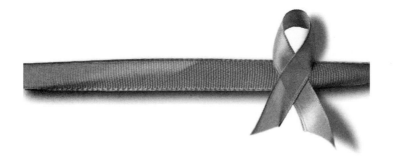

*B*e careful what you ask for, my mother always said, *you just might get it.* This was something that always perplexed me. "If I ask for something, Mom, why wouldn't I want it? If it came my way, what's the harm?"

In January, 2001, the year was starting out pretty well…so well in fact that I wondered and prayed to God about it. "Lord," I prayed, "why am I so blessed? I have a great husband, great kids, a great home, and a wonderful job. I feel like I'm not doing enough to deserve all this. Why me, Lord? Why did You choose me to have such a great life when so many others are suffering?"

Be careful what you pray for; you just may get the answer in a big way!

A few weeks later, I was enjoying a hot bubble bath and a good book. This ritual was my way of unwinding. I was so busy, I had put relaxing on my list of things to do just so I'd fit it in! This was a quiet, peaceful moment I savored. While I soaked in the warm water, I thought my breasts felt a little funny, but figured it must be because my period was coming on.

I also remembered that, while I was driving home earlier in the week, I had a familiar feeling in my right breast—as though it had filled up with milk. It was the same feeling I'd had while I was expecting my children. I had thought, *I can't be pregnant.*

As I lathered up, I noticed in my right breast a pea-sized lump. To the right of that was an egg-shaped mass. I'd always had lumpy, bumpy breasts. But there was something different about these two places. Trying to blow it off as probably nothing, I jumped into some flannel pajamas and turned the TV on to ABC 33/40 in Birmingham, the station where I anchor the 6 and 10 pm news. An "Oprah" rerun was on.

## A Message from Oprah

It was then that I remembered the Oprah show from a few nights before. Oprah's guest was a woman who had battled breast cancer while living at the South Pole. She had mentioned an egg-shaped mass. On that show, someone mentioned a deadly type of breast cancer that showed up as an egg-shaped mass and often traveled to the brain.

I began to worry and got a cold chill even with my warm flannels on. I told myself, *I'm overreacting. I should probably get my yearly check up soon anyway.*

Being a busy working mom, I put off calling the doctor for a few weeks. I told Doug Bell, my husband of 13 years, about the lump. He urged me to go check it out. I wanted him to say it was probably nothing.

I found ways to be too busy to rush to the doctor's office. I like to think of myself as an intelligent person, but delaying this doctor visit was not the brightest thing to do. Two weeks after I discovered the lump, I mentioned to Doug again that it was still there. He said. "Call Dr. Snowden today—it's probably nothing. Just get it checked out."

The important point about that conversation is that I only called because a loved one pushed me to do it. Don't worry about nagging someone you care about to go to the doctor. It's okay to nag for a good reason. Had Doug not urged me, I would have put it off or even forgotten about it. Had I not been watching Oprah on ABC 33/40 that night, I might not have been alarmed about the lumps. My husband, ABC 33/40, and Oprah all helped save my life! I called my doctor, Dr. Elizabeth Snowden, that day.

## *ABCs of Survival*

Dr. Snowden had become a friend over the years. She helped save our first baby's life when I had pre-term labor in the fifth month of pregnancy. She ordered me to bed for several weeks, and saw me through that crisis.

The good thing about that pregnancy scare is that the weeks I spent in bed helped me to prepare to be a mother. I had time to read my Bible. I also came up with my ABC survival tips. After I found the lump in my breast, those ABC survival tips were once again helpful. Here they are:

**A—Accept what you can't change.** *"Therefore I tell you, do not worry about your life, what you will* *eat or drink; or about your body, what you will wear. Is not life more important than food, and the body more important than clothes? Look at the birds of the air; they do not sow or reap or store away in barns, and yet our heavenly Father feeds them. Are you not much more valuable than they? Who of you by worrying can add a single hour to his life?"* —*Matthew 6:25–27.* You can't. Worrying only adds to your problems, and studies show it's bad for your immune system.

**B—Be your best for others.** Even while you're stuck in bed, you can be a great witness for the Lord. The story of Kareem McNeal inspires me. In the early '90s he was an offensive tackle for the University of Alabama football team. One night he and his cousin had a car accident. Kareem was thrown from the car, and his spinal cord was injured. The injury left him paralyzed. As he left the hospital, the statement he gave reporters shocked me. He said, "God has a plan for my life, and I want to help others." Wow, how powerful! This young man could have been angry and bitter, but he was a witness for the Lord. Years later I heard a story about a child who refused to get off a bus to go into the Rise program in Tuscaloosa. The Rise program is a school for children with special needs. Who was the only person able to get that scared child off the bus and into the school? Kareem McNeal. God had a plan, and Kareem did help others. *"O LORD Almighty, blessed is the man who trusts in you."* —*Psalm 84:12*

**C—Courage.** *"Have I not commanded you? Be strong and courageous. Do not be terrified; do not be discouraged, for the Lord your God will be with you wherever you go."*—*Joshua 1:9*. It was courage I needed then during my pre-term labor, and it was courage I would need for the next challenge in my life. While I was in bed for months, my faith became stronger, as did my friendship with Dr. Snowden. She carefully watched over me and did everything she could to make sure my baby wasn't born too early. Dr. Beth Snowden was my hero twice. First she saved the life of my baby, who is now eight years old, and now she was about to help save my life.

## The Breast Exam

I was on the exam table while Dr. Snowden performed one of those clinical breast exams that sort of tickles and hurts at the same time.

"Hmmm," she said. "The lump doesn't seem to be anything to worry about, but there has been a good deal of change in the breast tissue." I was impressed that she remembered what my breasts felt like a year ago. Hadn't she felt hundreds of other breasts since my last exam? She then suggested that I get a mammogram.

I said, "The area hurts a little. That's usually a cyst or something, isn't it?" I tried to reassure myself. I was relieved she didn't seem to think it was cancer.

I waited another week or two to get the mammogram. But then one day, I had a nagging feeling. Something wasn't right. Yes, I needed to go in and get that mammogram so I could get on with my life and put my question to rest.

Within a few days I was in the mammography room getting my breasts smashed between two pieces of plastic. Not my idea of a good time. Then to add insult to injury, the lab tech said, "I keep getting a wrinkle on that right breast." I had large breasts, and I assumed the changes were simply because I had had three children. The pleasant lab tech tried again to iron out the wrinkle in my breast and proceeded.

A few days later at 4:35 in the afternoon, less than two hours from news time, I got a call at my desk from the lab tech. She said, "We have your results. I can't tell you anything except your doctor will take good care of you. Your doctor just got the results this afternoon and will probably contact you very soon."

I felt like someone had just poured cold water through my veins. This didn't sound good. But again I assured myself this was nothing to worry about. I hung up the phone, and literally a few seconds later the phone rang again.

"This is Brenda," I answered.

"Brenda, this is Beth Snowden," my doctor said. I thought, *Uh-oh…this is bad.*

"Beth, how are you?" I said.

She always had a pleasant, soothing tone, but I sensed some worry in her voice. "I'm fine. I just got your results from your mammogram, and I'd like you to see a surgeon," she said.

At that point my mind was racing, and I kept thinking *this is nothing.* But I had a bad feeling about this one. That feeling of cold ice water in my veins wouldn't leave. I was shocked to hear I'd have to see a surgeon. I had always been the healthy one in the family! My parents had heart conditions, my sister had a heart condition, and another sister had diabetes.

"She's a really great doctor. I think you'll like her," Beth said. "Her name is Dr. Susan Winchester, and she's a Christian. She's really very nice."

Nice or not, she was still a surgeon, and I

didn't want to have to see her.

"Okay, when should I go? Next week?" I said.

"I'd like you to see her tomorrow," she said.

Tomorrow! That sounded pretty serious. This surgery was apparently so urgent that I couldn't put it off.

I hung up the phone, and tears welled in my eyes. I turned to my producer and friend Jamie Morrison and told her about the conversations. She was confident and reassured me. That day I did the 6 and 10 pm news and worked on special reports for the ratings period. Work was a welcome distraction from the worry of possibly having breast cancer.

The next morning my husband Doug and I were in the surgeon's office. It was packed with people. We were graciously escorted back to a break room complete with a light-colored pine table and four chairs, a refrigerator, and a microwave. The nurse had mercy on us, getting us out of the waiting room since we had both been local television personalities for many years. Often people would want to know why we were there, which is fine under any other circumstance. But the prospect of breast cancer, the thought of chatting lightly about it in a waiting room, was almost too much to bear.

## Meeting the Surgeon

While we waited, the quiet time alone with my husband was pretty nice. With three children and two demanding careers, any time alone is precious. So we talked and joked and I even got out what had been my Christmas present from Doug, my hand-held personal computer.

I showed him how much I'd been using it. He was amazed at all the options, including the games. At that moment, the doctor walked in to introduce herself.

"How do you like your palm pilot?" she asked.

"It's great," I replied.

She told us how much she'd been using her new device. A surgeon who likes the latest gadgets! I thought that was a good sign. Dr. Snowden was right; I did like this strong, confident woman. I just hoped I wouldn't have to get to know her that much more. I hoped she'd examine the breast and then send us chuckling on our way because it was nothing.

Then it was off with the top and bra and into a snazzy little white paper cover-up that opened in the front. I always think how funny it is that we clutch these little white garments so close because of our modesty, but in the end the doctor and nurse see your birthday suit. There are no more secrets. But it feels better to have something to clutch anyway.

My husband and I are great at joking during tense times, and we told each other again this was all a big mistake, and it would be nothing. The doctor walked in and did a clinical breast exam on the right side, a more painful one than I ever remember having, then the left side. Then she did a sonogram, right then and there in the office. In a few minutes she said, "Okay, this lump doesn't appear to be anything to worry about." *Whew,* I thought. *That's exactly what I wanted to hear...nothing to worry about.* She went on to say that in some cases, doctors would want to do a lumpectomy, which would entail removing a fourth of the breast. But she didn't want to do that just yet. She said, "Get dressed, I'll be back in a minute."

Whew! What a relief. After she left the room, I joked to Doug as I clutched my clothes to my chest, "Lumpectomy, fourth of my breast...I think not... let's get out of here!"

He said, "No kidding!" Then we both laughed.

## My Husband Doug

My husband is my best friend. We've known each other for about 20 years. Looking at him during this moment when I thought we had just dodged a major bullet, I remembered what a carefree couple we had been in Gainesville, Florida, when we worked together at TV 20. I know God led me right to him.

Before I met Doug Bell, I worked in Tampa, Florida, at a family-operated TV station. We were shocked one day to be told we had been replaced by CNN! I thought that was my darkest day. I'd just lost my first job. I felt like a horse kicked me in the gut; the wind had been knocked out of me. I had just gotten out of college, and my Dad had retired from the steel industry. I was too proud to ask my parents for money at that point. A friend at TV-28 in Tampa suggested I apply for a job in Gainesville. The news director granted me an interview at the request of our mutual friend.

The day I drove from Tampa to Gainesville for the interview was a stormy spring day. When I arrived at TV-20, I stepped out of the car and into an ankle-deep puddle in my gray high heels. I fought to put my umbrella up and a gust of wind turned it inside-out. I ran for the door. So much for my first impression.

The news director was Mike Dotson, a friendly man with a beard and a deep raspy voice. He walked me through a wood-paneled hallway to the modest newsroom. Within a few seconds of walking into the newsroom, I was introduced to a tall, blond, blue-eyed, good-looking guy. Mike Dotson said, "Well, Doug, say something." Doug tripped over his words, almost tripped over his own feet, and said, "Hi."

I was so tickled and thought, *There's something different about that guy.* But enough daydreaming; I had a job to get. After the interview, I got the offer I was waiting for—a reporter's position with some fill-in anchoring. I was moving from Tampa to Gainesville! Little did I know that one of the worst things in my life, losing a job, would lead to one of my greatest blessings—Doug. God was definitely in charge.

Doug and I quickly became best friends. I remember talking with him in his red Camaro on the way to a local barbecue restaurant. Somehow the subject of religion and our backgrounds came up. It was almost eerie to find out we were both of English, Scotch-Irish descent with a little German thrown in for good measure. That led us to the question of religion. We had that in common, too. We were both raised Baptist. Was this a match made in heaven? I know it was. When I met his grandmother for the first time, she said she had been praying for someone like me to come along. Little did she know I had been praying for someone like him to come along, too! He was, and still is, the love of my life, a sensitive, caring, loving, and funny guy.

## The Bubble Burst

My warm fuzzy bubble of reflection burst when Dr. Winchester came back into the room. She had more news, and not what I wanted to hear. I was confused; I thought minutes before she had told us the lump was nothing to worry about. She wanted to see the results of my last mammogram. My last mammogram had been taken at ABC 33/40.

Our general manager, Roy Clem, and several caring people came up with the idea of providing free mammograms for employees and reduced-cost mammograms for the public. A local hospital brought the mobile mammography unit to the station. A friend, Vicki Hurn, pushed me to get a mammogram. She said, "Brenda, if you get this mammogram, others will follow you." So I went ahead with it. It was a good thing I did. Dr. Winchester wanted to see those results to compare to my latest results.

After studying the previous mammogram, Dr. Winchester said, "See, less than a year ago you had a normal mammogram. But in this recent one, look at these little white spots. These spots could be calcification, which is a normal part of the aging process, or they could be cancer. It's not the lump but the little white spots that we're concerned about."

Later that week I was scheduled for a steriotactic breast biopsy. It's more involved than your average needle biopsy. This little procedure involves a much bigger needle. It's about the width of a key and seemed as long as one of those do-it-yourself car wash tools. But the good news is that it provides a sample of tissue for the pathologist without requiring a lumpectomy. The scar is minute compared to the one left behind from a lumpectomy, which can leave a woman's breast disfigured.

I walked into the room, and a cheerful physician's assistant named Charla tried to put me at ease. She explained that I'd lie facedown on the table with my breast protruding through a hole in the table, and the surgeon, like a car mechanic, would work from beneath me. The doctor would then use the instrument to retrieve breast tissue for the pathologist to analyze. As I looked at the cushioned table I thought, *this should include a massage and a pedicure while I'm lying around.* As I tried to get comfortable on the table while allowing my breast to drop through the hole, I asked, "So what's my chance or percentage...how many people who get these biopsies actually have cancer?"

Charla responded, "Oh, it's low, about fifteen percent."

Dr. Winchester explained that she would insert the instrument into the breast tissue, then pull some tissue out, then insert a metal tag so they could watch the area in the future. The instrument has painkiller on it to numb the area as it goes into the tissue. She said, "Ready," and I braced myself and heard what was like the pop of a gun. It was a little painful, but not all that bad. She took one sample, then another and another.

There was one area where the painkiller hadn't numbed the tissue yet, and I yelled, "Yow!" But it was amazing—within a matter of seconds more numbing medicine was inserted and I could stand the procedure for a few more minutes.

I'm a very intuitive person, and that can be good or bad at times. As the nurse took my breast tissue samples to a pathologist to read, I had one of those bad feelings. What seemed like a decade later, the nurse came back, and she had a look on her face. Either she had just gotten some bad news from home or I was about to get some bad news.

"Okay, Brenda, get dressed and then we'll talk," said Dr. Winchester.

I wondered how many times she's said that

phrase to patients. *Get dressed and then we'll talk.* Probably thousands of times.

Charla bandaged me and told me to keep a tight-fitting bra on for the next couple of days and not to exercise. The areas where they retrieved the tissue could fill up with blood, and that would be even more painful. Dr. Winchester returned and pointed once again to the white spots on the mammogram. I heard her words but they weren't making any sense to me. Finally I said, "You mean it's not benign?"

"No," She said.

The next question seems dumb, but I was dumbfounded at this point. "Is it cancer?" I said.

"Yes. It's definitely not benign and it is a form of cancer, but we're not sure how far along it is yet." A cold chill went up my spine and I was trembling. I asked the same question about six times. "Are you sure it's cancer, are you sure it's not benign?" The answer was the same each time. Dr. Winchester had dealt with shocked patients before. She was very calm and comforting. Thoughts hit me...*Am I going to die? How long do I have? Can I beat this? What about the children?* My dear sweet husband didn't know yet.

I called Doug on his cell phone to see if he could come to the doctor's office. He had just interviewed a basketball coach and was already on his way. He asked, "Is everything okay?"

"Oh sure," I lied. I didn't want him to crash while getting the news by cell phone. "But Dr. Winchester wants to meet with both of us," I said. I hoped I was convincing. When he arrived, I felt like my knight in shining armor was by my side. I buried my face in his chest and was thankful for the much-needed hug.

Dr. Winchester delicately explained that the white spots on the mammogram were, in fact, cancer. I continued to tremble. As I shook, Charla stood behind me and patted my back. I was glad she was creating a diversion, because I wanted to hide my trembling from Doug. I felt I needed to be strong for my husband. He was also getting the shock of his life. He didn't understand at first and asked the same questions about six times, just as I had. Dr. Winchester repeated the words "mastectomy is in order." I certainly didn't want a mastectomy, but I didn't want cancer growing inside my body either. I knew I had to do anything I could to beat the cancer for the sake of my three little boys and my husband. The word *cancer* rang in my head, and again, I wondered, *Am I going to die?*

Dr. Winchester assured us that we'd caught it early and there was a very good chance they would get all the cancer out and I could go on to live a normal life.

The diagnosis also meant our much-needed family vacation to Disney was off, and surgery was to be scheduled for the next week. I hated the thought of telling the boys.

Dr. Winchester suggested we meet the next day because she would know more about the extent of the cancer after another pathologist read the results.

More thoughts raced through my mind as Doug and I left the office. Would he still love me after all this? How would he feel? Would the kids be okay?

## Telling People

I was stunned. I remember walking to my car in shock. I was getting in the car to head to work. How surreal and bizarre.

"Doug, I'll have to tell (my boss) Garry Kelly and (my general manager) Roy Clem. We're in the middle of ratings!" That's our report card. Each night for one month several times a year we are "graded" by how many viewers tune in.

He said, "Okay, honey, it'll be alright; we'll get through this." We hugged gently (I was still sore from the biopsy), kissed, and parted. I was on my way to inform my boss and friend of five years that I had cancer.

Garry Kelly, my friendly, caring boss, has a beard and a full head of silver hair. "Garry," I said, "I have breast cancer. I have to have surgery, and hopefully I won't need chemo, but they won't know that until after the operation. The doctor has to see how far the cancer has spread. If it's in the lymph nodes, then I'll have to have chemo, and probably lose my hair."

Garry said, "If you have to go in tonight, you go. Ratings are nothing compared to your life." We were in February ratings. No one is excused unless there's a life-threatening situation or a death in the family. On this day I felt like both had happened. Cancer was certainly life-threatening, but part of me had already died. I had lived my life thinking I was a healthy person and would always be a healthy person. This diagnosis caused my bubble to burst, and what I thought of as the invincible part of me died, in a sense.

On the way home from work, I called my big sister Linda, who is a nurse. While she was valiant, I could tell I knocked her for a loop. I asked her to help me tell Mom and Dad. They both had heart conditions. She agreed to help ease the shock as best she could. "And," she said, "I'm coming up to help you." Normally, I'd say no, I'm okay, don't spend the money, I don't want to burden you. But I jumped at her offer.

"That would be great," I said. "Thank you!" I was glad to have my smart, strong sister to help me.

Doug also had to make the call to his parents. "Mom, Brenda has breast cancer," he informed her. Those words stung me. Usually when he talked to his parents, he'd boast, Brenda did this, Brenda did that. Brenda won an Associated Press award. But this was no award. I almost felt ashamed that I was sick. I felt I was letting everyone down—my family, my friends, my colleagues. I thought to myself, *those doubts have to stop. I need all my energy to fight this thing.*

Before Doug hung up the phone, his parents were planning the trip to our house. Linda was coming to help me, and grandparents would help with the children. I called friends to make carpool arrangements. All that was in place.

## Emotions and Prayer

Now I had to deal with all the information that was thrown at me. I was studying breast cancer and cramming for the exam of my life. I read as many books as I could. I had to make the right decisions.

As I was reading the material from Dr.

Winchester, I found a note from one of the nuns at St. Vincent's Hospital. It talked about the emotions people go through after a cancer diagnosis. They were the same emotions people experience when there's a death in the family. First there's shock, disbelief, denial, anger, and finally acceptance.

I was definitely in the shock part. I prayed that this wasn't really cancer, that I would be healed, but most of all I prayed to live and to be able to raise my children. I asked the Lord to watch over us. I did something I had never done before; I prayed for my own health. I thought how over the years I prayed for the health of my children, my husband, my parents and in-laws, but I never once prayed for my own health. From that day on, I included prayer for my own health.

But as I prayed *let this all be a mistake,* I felt like a child making a request that was being refused by a parent. Even though I prayed, I knew the answer deep down. This was cancer, and I would have to accept it.

## The Pathologist's Report

I hoped that the pathologist's report would show the cancer was in the very earliest stage. The morning after the biopsy, Dr. Winchester called us with the pathologist's results. She told us the cancer was farther along than she first thought. Instead of my cancer being ductal carcinoma in situ, it was invasive ductal carcinoma, which meant it was no longer contained in the milk ducts. It had spread outside the milk ducts, and there was a chance it had spread to the lymph nodes under my arm. From there the cancer can spread to other parts of the body.

Dr. Winchester explained, "Depending on how big the tumor is, we'll decide if you'll need chemotherapy." But they couldn't know for sure until I had surgery and they dissected my lymph nodes. Lymph nodes are amazing little parts of our bodies. These are little body-cleansing sacs that often try to catch the cancer before it can spread. Hopefully they catch all the cells and prevent a recurrence.

Dr. Winchester also talked about reconstruction, about rebuilding the body. She said, "I want you to meet Dr. Beckenstein. He's a very talented plastic surgeon who can reconstruct the breast." It was welcome news; after hearing my body would be cut apart, there was hope that I could be put back together again. Doug and I went to Dr. Michael Beckenstein's office, and a few minutes later he walked into the room with a friendly smile. His comfortable way made us like him instantly.

As I clutched Doug's hand, Dr. Beckenstein explained the options I would have after the mastectomy. I could go with a straight implant, or I could undergo something called the tram flap procedure. That's where you get a tummy tuck and they use the extra muscle and tissue to rebuild the breast area. I could use tissue from my stomach or back or rear. But he added that people sometimes have discomfort sitting down after using tissue from the rear. I could imagine they would!

We watched a videotape about the process, and then it was time for me to be examined again. I thought to myself, *How many people will see my birthday suit before we're through?* The doctor looked at my breasts as if he were a sculptor and I was the clay. He explained that he would ask the surgeon to make the incision under the breast and then cut up the middle part of the breast. This way the scars would look like a simple tummy tuck and breast reduction. Traditionally, the incision is made in an oval around the nipple. Then he pinched my stomach skin and pushed on it. "Hmmm," he said, "there may not be enough tissue here to do the tram flap. Your stomach is protruding a bit, but that's a weakened abdominal wall from having babies." He urged me not to lose any weight in the meantime.

"No problem, I'll go on a strict high-fat diet to

pump up my tummy as best I can," I said. I got dressed and he handed me brochures on my way out. I had plenty of homework to do. I had a lot of decisions to make.

It was an unbelievable few days! Not only did I have to digest the fact that I had cancer, and that this disease could end my life, and that I had to get a mastectomy, but now I had to make decisions about how I'd be put back together.

# Chapter Three

# On to Surgery

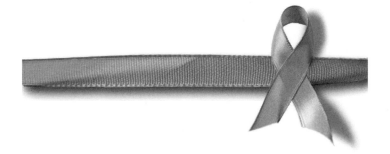

*I* decided soon after I was diagnosed that I had to share this news with others. If I felt this good, I thought to myself, and I had cancer growing inside of me, I have to warn others. There were other mothers, sisters, and daughters out there with a killer growing inside of them…and they didn't even know it. My sweet protective husband and caring doctors suggested I wait until after the surgery and chemo treatments to go public. But there wasn't much time to waste; we had to start spreading the word right away to save lives.

Out of respect to my husband, I told him going public had to be our decision together. Since we are a team, this affected him in a big way, too, and I knew he had to deal with a deluge of emotions just as I did. I wanted to settle the issue of going public with the news. I remember sitting in the driveway, praying for God to lead us to the right decision together. Doug was at his office. He worked for a sports cable network. I called him and said, "Honey, I really feel led to go public."

He said, "I don't know honey...let me think about this." Doug was always good about thinking things through. I, on the other hand, could make a snap decision and run with it. We were a good balance that way.

I prayed again after hitting the end button on my cell phone. And no kidding, a minute later he called back and said "Okay, let's go public."

God was working in this from the beginning.

Do I regret going public? I wondered if I would. I didn't know how people would react. But I've received only more blessings from sharing my diagnosis with viewers.

That day I marched into my news director's office and said, "We decided. I want to tape an announcement about my breast cancer to be aired the day of surgery. But I want it done right, with good lighting so that I don't look sick." In reality, I didn't feel sick at all.

Garry said, "Are you sure?"

"Yes," I said, determined that there was no going back.

Both Garry and General Manager Roy Clem assured me that if I decided at anytime not to air the announcement, they would pull it, even if it was right before news time. The kindness I felt from my two superiors was incredible. My bosses and co-workers became like a close-knit family for me.

Jamie Morrison, the producer for the "Fighting for You" consumer segment I did each week, became like a sister. After I told her I was on a high fat diet for the next week until surgery, she brought me homemade chocolate peanut butter balls. "Perfect," I said, and I kept them at my desk and nibbled on them throughout the afternoon. Jamie helped keep me laughing that week. That's a good friend.

Then I had to tell my other co-workers. Stephanie Brooks, the photographer who normally shoots my "Fighting for You" reports, is a pretty young lady with auburn hair and big blue eyes. "Hey Steph," I said, "I have to tell you something. I want you to hear it from me and not through the grapevine. I have breast cancer." To my surprise, I wasn't crying. I was okay! Dr. Winchester told me that when I could look someone in the face and say I have breast cancer and not cry about it I'd know I'd come to terms with it. But instead of me crying, tears were rolling down Stephanie's cheeks. "I'll be off for a number of weeks, so you hold down the fort for me, okay?"

When I told my co-anchor, Josh Thomas, his body moved backward suddenly as if reacting to the sound of a gun. I explained that I was going to share the news with viewers, so he might need to answer some questions. He agreed to do whatever he could, and I appreciated that.

James Spann, our meteorologist, is highly respected and well known as a Christian in our community. I told him I was going public with the news, and he said, "This is your mission." And it remains my mission, to warn people about cancer and ease the blow in some small way.

When I told Mike Raita, our sports director, he just said, "No, this can't be true!"

"I wish it wasn't, Mike," I said. "But it is, and I'm going to fight it."

Just as I took friends aside at work to tell them I had breast cancer, I also phoned my dearest friends. I didn't want them to find out about this on the six o'clock news.

## Telling the World

The next project was to write and tape my announcement for the day of surgery. Imagine trying to come up with a script telling the world you have breast cancer. I consulted with Liz Hurley, a news anchor in Huntsville, Alabama, who had also had breast cancer and lost her mother to the disease as a child. She urged me to be honest, real, and to tell it like it is. I sat at my desk and tapped away at the keyboard and wrote the most important message of my life. This announcement aired on the six o'clock news while I was still in surgery:

*My husband saved my life, and here's how. About a month ago I felt a lump in my breast, and at the urging of my husband I had a mammogram. While the lump I found turned out to be nothing to worry about, the doctor found an early form of breast cancer. She had a previous mammogram to compare it to, one that I had right here at ABC 33/40 less than a year before. It clearly showed there were major breast changes. That led to a biopsy and diagnosis that I did have breast cancer. My doctor believes we caught the cancer early, and with surgery doctors say the odds are in my favor. I have a very good chance of getting rid of it.*

*Right now I am either still in surgery, or I've just gotten out of surgery. I plan to meet this latest challenge in my life head on and fight. And fight for your health as well by urging women to do breast self-exams and to get mammograms, and men to get cancer screenings. This silent disease struck me and I had no clue it was invading my body. Right now, I feel just fine. That's why regular checks for cancer are so important. Remember, early detection is the key. If my sharing my diagnosis saves one life, then it will be worth everything I'm going through. Early detection is the key to survival. Together we can do battle with a killer and win. And with the help of my doctors, family, friends, and faith, it will be okay.*

*Fighting for you, Brenda Ladun, ABC 33/40.*

Then my co-anchor Josh Thomas announced that instead of sending flowers, donations could be made to the Susan G. Komen Breast Cancer Foundation. He also announced that ABC 33/40 was providing free mammograms in my honor through a local hospital. The next Saturday, more than a hundred women got free mammograms at the St. Vincent's Mammography Center located inside a department store at a local shopping center.

Getting Better, Not Bitter

I didn't know how people would react to my announcement of my cancer diagnosis and treatment. I guess I didn't think about it; there was no time that week to think about anything except getting myself and my family prepared for the surgery.

## The Surgery

The morning of surgery, I kept thinking about several Bible verses. Proverbs 3:5 rolled around in my head: "Trust in the Lord with all your heart and lean not on your own understanding."

At 5:30 in the morning on February 26, 2001, I was mentally preparing to go into surgery. I gave Doug my miracle medal, which my friend Lisa Baggett had given me. It is a Catholic medal that represents hope. Even though we're Baptists and don't know much about Catholic medals, it made me feel better knowing my friend and her church were praying for us. Doug held it for me—he put it on that day and has worn it ever since.

I remember taking off my clothes and jewelry and putting them in a bag. I had to give it all up. It was just me, my hospital gown, and God going into surgery together. The thought ran through my mind, *You can't take it with you.* Putting my watch in the bag, I thought how prisoners must feel when they have to give everything up.

A nurse came into the room with a number of consent forms and a living will form. I had to sign something that had to do with me living or dying. I also filled out a form that stated the tissue could be used in a research study. I now realize that with each bit of help researchers can get, the closer we are to a cure.

Just then to my surprise, our pastor, Buddy Gray, came into the room. He asked if he could pray with us. I was so grateful he came. It was a welcome surprise. He also said how the Lord works in wonderful ways. At 5:45 that morning, he had run into another church member in the parking lot. That man's wife was also having a mastectomy that day, but they hadn't told anyone. Buddy was able to pray with her before surgery. He said, "If you weren't here, I wouldn't be here for them." I thought, *Well there's something good that's come out of this already.* We prayed, and I felt a sense of peace.

Something else wonderful happened before dawn on the day of my surgery. This type-A personality, who had to be in control and make the house, the kids, the husband, the career, even the dog run smoothly, had to let go. I realized I was not really in control of anything. God was in control. What a freeing feeling! God was in control of everything in my life. On this morning of major surgery, I put all the worry and fear on Him, and allowed the Lord to take away my fear. I felt as if He wrapped His arms around me.

God really was in control that day. When Dr. Winchester opened me up, she found a lot more cancer in my right breast than was revealed by the mammogram. She asked Doug if he would consent to a double mastectomy. She said if not, it was very likely that I would have a recurrence on the other side in six months to a year. Doug made the right decision on that day. As he put it, it was the only decision.

I was in surgery for thirteen hours. Waking up in the recovery room, I felt like I was in one of those television commercials where you get a limited view—the camera isn't really going where you want it to go. My cameras, my eyes, could only open and I could barely move my head. I remember hearing my husband's voice, but I couldn't focus on him.

"Bren! Bren! You look good!" he said as he kissed me. Even under heavy sedation, I knew he was just saying that to make this lump of human flesh feel better about things.

I couldn't really see Doug, but I could see my hands. They were puffy and yellow. I later found out that the yellow came from a dye they pumped into my body to allow the plastic surgeon to better be able to see to connect tissue and arteries. My whole body was as puffy as a boxer's face after the twelfth round. Dr. Beckenstein moved into my field of vision and said, "Everything went well." It was good to hear. Then all I could think of was going back to sleep.

## Recovery

I remember several distinct things after waking up in my room, and they are common experiences for mastectomy patients.

I remember a tall, handsome male nurse explaining the benefits of the morphine pump. When the pain got unbearable, I could medicate myself. It was fuzzy, but I understood from him that if I hit the button with my thumb, a certain amount of morphine would be released. Every six minutes, I was allowed to push the pump, so I did. I didn't want to be a hero.

I remember my mother would go to the dentist and refuse any pain medicine. I also heard stories of my great-great-grandmother, who would stick the dentist with her hatpin if he hurt her. The women in my family are a spunky bunch, don't you think?

Again to add insult to injury, I noticed that I had begun my period! The nurse's assistant said that sometimes the surgery causes the period to start. I had to keep myself from laughing (that would have hurt!) when the nurse's assistant said with a thick southern accent, "I don't do tampons!"

Almost every hour the nurse would come in to press on the newly reconstructed breasts to make sure the tissue was "taking." These first few hours were crucial. It was like transplanting a plant. Most of the time it "takes." But once in awhile it doesn't. My plastic surgeon had prepared me; in the event the tissue didn't take and it died, then we'd have to do more surgery.

When I was taken off the morphine and started my pain medication, I noticed my mouth felt like it had been burned. My sister, the nurse, explained that was probably from the oxygen they pumped into my mouth during surgery. After thirteen hours it can burn. For two weeks, I still felt like it had been scalded by a cup of too-hot hot chocolate.

The other thing I had to deal with was incredible itching. The nurse said it had something to do with the drugs I had during surgery. My sister suspected it was a reaction to the morphine. The kind nurse who offered to scratch my back with my brush was an angel from heaven!

The day after surgery, the nurse came into my room and announced it was time to get up and go to the bathroom. *Are you crazy?* I thought to myself. *Do you know what they just did to me?* She instructed me to swing my legs to the side of the bed. I looked down and saw my foot shaking because I was so weak. I thought, *Hey, this isn't my body! Who took my body? I want my body back!*

For the first few days, my sweet husband Doug didn't leave my side. He helped pull me up out of bed. He was there to help me shuffle to the bathroom for the first time. Doug's strong arm was there for me to hold onto, and he steadied me. As Dr. Beckenstein had warned, I was walking like a hunchback.

Doug actually subscribed to the "laughter is the best medicine" theory at this point. He chided me about being a hunchback. I laughed and whoa! I wanted to smack him for causing the stitches to hurt so badly. Those jokes continued for weeks and are the reason I straightened up in record time, according to my doctors. I guess laughter really is the best medicine! After I settled back in the hospital bed, I looked at Doug. He looked as if he'd lost ten pounds in the last twenty-four hours. He looked skinny and his face was drawn, with dark circles under his eyes.

Getting Better, Not Bitter

"I know what happened to me, but what happened to you?" I joked, careful not to really laugh because it would really hurt. Those first days after surgery, I imagined Doug with a big S on his shirt. While he spent a lot of time at the hospital with me, he'd also dash home to make sure the kids were reassured. We both knew they were in good hands with Grandma, Grandpa, and Vanessa Echols, our long-time nanny (whom we call "Nessa"), but he wanted to support them emotionally, too.

Dear friends came to visit and sent cards and flowers. One gift in particular made me chuckle. It was a refrigerator magnet with a picture of a cat flat on its back, with the words, "I'm fine, really!" That's what I kept saying to the friends and co workers who came to see me, although I couldn't fool anyone in my drugged and puffy state.

My sister Linda arrived three days after my surgery. I was glad to see her. Linda would take control of everything and make it right. Seeing her was like drinking a nice cup of hot tea. She soothed me.

Linda came just in time to relieve Doug. He needed a break, and I insisted that he continue life as normal as possible and go to the Big 12 basketball tournament. After all, my sister was there, and Grandma and Grandpa were at home with Nessa to take care of the kids.

# Going Home

The day that I'd prayed for came; it was time to go home. But I panicked at the thought. I could just see me standing in the doorway holding my drains, hunched over and shuffling, as the boys all ran to tackle me. *Ahh, maybe I need another day*, I thought. *I want to walk in that door and be strong and be Mommy again. I don't want to scare my own children with this frail, weak body.* I started to cry, and then one of the wonderful compassionate nurses asked me what was wrong. I told her, and apparently she ratted on me to Dr. Beckenstein. He came in later and said, "I heard you broke down and cried today. What's going on?" I later found out the nurse probably reported my tears to the doctor because depression can be a serious side effect after surgery. I explained that I was afraid, and he assured me that I'd heal faster at home. After talking to him I felt less scared.

Next, I had to figure out what the latest fashion was for a hospital exit, complete with drains. My sister Linda came to the rescue again and gave me one of her button-down-the-front shirts, and a sweater. It was perfect. While I was weak, in pain, and sluggish from the medication, just figuring out what to wear felt like a major undertaking. When I arrived home, the children were in school and Garret was napping. I was greeted by my in-laws and Nessa, our nanny. It was a long walk from the car to the bed. When I finally reached the bed, I collapsed. It was good to be home again. I was exhausted. But I'd entered an important phase of my recovery...convalescing at home. Those first few days, I slept a lot. I imagined that after each nap, I'd healed just a little more. And that was what my life was about at that point...healing. It was time to start healing physically, mentally, and spiritually.

*Chapter Four*

# Chemo Moments

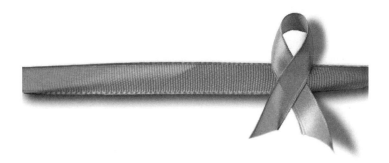

Because the pathologists found microscopic disease in two lymph nodes, chemotherapy was
recommended. Chemo is sort of like an extermina-
tor to stamp out any little cancerous cells that might
be left in my body.

When I met my oncologist, Dr. Cantrell, for the
first time, I felt like a deer in headlights. I knew I
should be more scared of what recurring cancer
could do to me, but for some reason I was even

more scared of the chemo than I had been of the surgery. I couldn't comprehend much of what he was saying, except that if I did the chemo, I'd have a good chance of never seeing a recurrence. This was, in fact, a battle plan. But was the fear of the chemo worse than actually going through it?

During the 6 pm news I gave updates of my ongoing treatment and also produced a one-hour special on the cancer experience called "Cancer: A New Horizon." I shared my fear of chemo with my viewers as I walked them through the next phase in the fight. Here's the report on chemotherapy I gave to my viewers:

*Seven weeks ago, I had surgery for breast cancer and shared that with you to remind you to keep a check on your own health. Now, that battle continues and, as we promised, we'll continue to walk you through the process. For the next few weeks, I'll tell you about my fight to show you how life goes on. Before I began chemotherapy, I wondered if the dread of it was worse than the actual experience. So far, that's turned out to be true. I feared the worst but learned I could make it.*

The director then rolled the story.
*Breast cancer. First came the diagnosis.*

**Doug Bell:** *It was like somebody punched me in the solar plexus.*

**Brenda:** *I remember trembling as I listened to the surgeon after the biopsy in this room. She said it was cancer. Our spring break vacation to Disney was off and a mastectomy had to be scheduled.*

**Doug:** *I was shocked, then I looked at you…you had that look of determination and you wanted to tackle it, so it made me feel a lot better.*

**Brenda:** *Together we fielded one of life's curve balls. And it felt like I was on a rollercoaster, trying to gather information and make all the right decisions. A little more than a week after the diagnosis, I was in surgery for a mastectomy.*

**Doug:** *After the initial surgery, Dr. Winchester came in and said the cancer was more widespread than they first thought.*

**Brenda:** *My husband and my doctor decided I'd have a better chance of beating the cancer with a double mastectomy.*

**Doug:** *The chances of the same thing happening in the left breast were pretty good. I knew it was the best thing for you. It was really the only decision.*

**Brenda:** *But even with the double mastectomy, I still had about a 50 percent chance of the cancer appearing somewhere else in my body because it had spread to the lymph nodes. That's why the next* *step in the fight had to be fought with chemothera-py.*

**Brenda:** *This is one of the baddest of the bad boys in the chemo line—adriamycin. Some people call this one the red devil. Hopefully it will seek out and kill any cancer cells floating around the body. The allied forces of chemo drugs adriamycin, cytoxan, and taxol will give me a more than fighting chance. The worst part of the treatment is getting a PICC (peripherally inserted central venous catheter) line in the arm from the initial needle. The battle is on because once the breast cancer cells attach to anoth-er organ and form a tumor, it's a whole different ballgame.*

*The plan of attack included adriamycin, which comes from a fungus, cytoxan, which was devel-oped from a chemical warfare substance—it's a cousin to mustard gas, and taxol, which comes from the leaves of a yew tree.*

*Remember, without the treatment I'd have about a 50 percent chance of a recurrence. But with this treatment and a five-year cancer prevention drug, my chance of seeing a recurrence is 8 percent or less. That's a chance I can live with, even if it means I'll lose my hair because of the chemo drugs.*

**Dr. Cantrell:** *That will be lethal for the cancer cell*

*and not for the patient…although it may be lethal for some of your other cells like your hair follicles. But it is not permanently lethal. With adriamycin, you will lose your hair.*

[Video of Brenda trying on wig]
**Brenda:** *But that's why they make wigs. You can buy hair, and it's only temporary. The other symptoms are nausea and fatigue.*

[Brenda at home holding medicine bottles.]
*I take this medication for nausea, this is a steroid for energy, and this helps prevent infections. Then every now and then, I have to take a rest and say, "See ya, guys."*

[Video of cheese crackers]
*But even with the anti-nausea medication…when that sick feeling creeps in during the day, cheese crackers help fend it off.*

[chemotherapy video]
*The other thing the doctor must watch closely is the white cell count. Those white cells fend off disease; chemotherapy and cancer lower those counts and leave the patient open to infections.*

[video of Brenda at work on the phone]
*This week I passed my test. The white count is just high enough so that I will be allowed to continue working* [video of me playing with children] *and playing.*

*The rule is that I must rest when I feel I need it. My new regimen includes more naps, less stress, enjoying every moment as it comes, and of course, more prayer.*

**Doug:** *Brenda's one of the strongest people I know; small in stature, but strong. Does that come from faith? I think so!*

[Brenda on set]
**Brenda:** *My family, faith, and friends continue to give me strength. A special thanks to my husband Doug for being my knight in shining armor throughout this fight. By the way, the dread of chemo was worse than the actual treatment.*

What I should have included in that report was the fact that I really appreciated my husband's company at the treatments. One day, they even had an open room with a bed and a chair. On that day we were granted the opportunity to be together, almost alone in the room, with the exception of the chemo nurse who would come in and administer the drugs and chemo into my veins. That couple of hours he sat with me and we got a chance to talk, joke,and just be together. That was the upside of having chemo that day.

## After Chemo Treatment

I'd heard that for some people, eating lunch right after treatment helped. For me it seemed to. A nice salad and a hot bowl of French onion soup seemed to soothe me. I'd come home and lay down for thirty minutes or an hour before getting up and going to work. I just wanted life to be normal. Going to work was normal. I didn't want to let anyone down. That's why I kept trudging along. There were many days I felt like I was in a fog and tired beyond belief. I remember the fatigue after the first chemo treatment. I came home to have dinner with Doug and the children, and after eating a few bites I said, "I'm just going to lay down for 10 minutes." Thirty-five minutes later Doug rustled me from what felt like a deep sleep.

"Are you going to go back to work?" he asked.

I jumped up like a school kid who just heard the school bus honking in front of the house. My heart pounded and I felt like I was moving in slow motion, trying to shake off the fatigue. I kissed everyone goodbye and hopped in the car to go back to work. The nausea hit me at the red light just before I got on the highway. I had the medicine Dr. Cantrell gave me, but I wondered what its side effects might be. As I neared the TV station, ten minutes away, the nausea was rising to a crescendo.

I made it to my desk and called the nurse on call. I wanted to be sure it was okay to take this medicine and drive back home.

I'm glad I checked that night. Dr. Cantrell called me back to ask how I was doing.

I said, "Dr. Cantrell, I think I might need to take one of the anti-nausea pills you prescribed. But I just wanted to know if it would be okay to take before the news."

He said with a chuckle, "If you take that medicine, you may not make it to do the news...you might be singing the news!"

"Okay," I said, "that answers my question. I have to drive home, too. I guess I'll try to hold off."

I hung up and thought, oh no, this is getting worse, not better. Then I thought of the cheese cracker method of nausea control I had heard about from Helen Dickinson. She's the teacher and neighbor who had breast cancer a year before me.

I reached into the cabinet above my desk and grabbed the cheese crackers. It was worth a try; at

8:35 pm I didn't have much time to decide whether or not I could go on. It was getting so bad, soon I knew I'd be in the bathroom vomiting. I chomped on one cracker. It didn't help. Then I tried another and I thought there was a bit of leveling off of the nausea. So I ate a third cracker. It was better! I wasn't perfect, but I knew I wouldn't horrify the viewing audience by getting sick all over the desk. Thank you, Helen, you saved us all an embarrassing moment.

I did push the envelope during chemo. I walked to keep my strength. Many of those beautiful spring days I was accompanied by Nessa, our nanny, and baby Garrett. I couldn't lift Garrett yet, and Nessa came along for a chat and a walk. I enjoyed our walks and talks. Her stories took my mind off of cancer. It was refreshing. Another cancer patient agreed with me that the walking helped keep the energy level up.

## *The Chemo Community*

What's good about sitting around for a couple of hours getting chemotherapy or poison pumped into your arm? Making friends with people who are traveling the same path you are on. These are people dealing with the same scary statistics, uncertainties, and pain. They really can understand. On one of those visits for chemo, I met a sweet lady with whom I instantly felt a bond. Her name is Francis Farmer. We started talking about what helped beat the side effect of chemotherapy. We were excited to find out that walking had a similar effect for us. It helped our energy levels and also helped fend off the nausea. Francis still calls to check on me, and I embrace her calls. I'm inspired to know she's doing okay and the cancer has stayed away. She breathes a sigh of relief for me, too. I ask her to stay in touch, and I know she will.

We really do have a team. The survivors help cheer each other on. Walking into the cancer center can be like a team meeting, even a pep rally. These are many of the same people I see week after week or month after month. I am so encouraged by the story of a woman with advanced-stage breast cancer. She had been given only a matter of months to live. But she proudly told me with a twinkle in her eye, almost like a child that got away with something, that that had been four years ago, and the cancer was under control. The treatments were working! There is such hope there in the waiting room.

I looked around and didn't see sick people. I saw survivors! These people were giving it their all to beat a killer. People in the waiting room would chat like long lost friends. One particular day, the daughter of the woman with the advanced-stage breast cancer walked over to an elderly man. She chatted with him and then went to retrieve a cup of cold water for him. At first I thought they were related. But after hearing them talk, I realized this was just another friendship made at the cancer center. *Too bad we couldn't all meet under more pleasant circumstances*, I thought. But no, we wouldn't have the bond we have now.

That's something cancer can do: it can bring people together or drive them apart. That can be an individual's choice. But reaching out and allowing someone to help you through is one way to cope and live through what seems impossible.

# Chapter Five

# *Getting Better, Not Bitter*

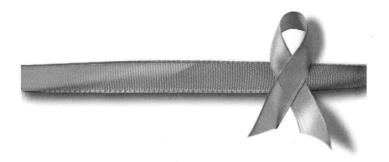

$\mathcal{M}$y breast cancer diagnosis wasn't just one big blow…it was several. Just when I thought I'd adjusted to the news, something else popped up to worry about. First came the diagnosis, the biopsy, the surgery, and now came the news that I had to watch for something called lymphedema. It's a swelling of the arm that can happen when the flow of the lymph system is interrupted. After the surgery I had about a month to heal before I began chemotherapy. I was mortified. I cried as I prayed that it wouldn't rob me of my life as I knew it. Chemotherapy is famous for sending patients to bed with fatigue and nausea. I also cried when I realized I was going to lose my hair. Blow after blow, the hits kept landing. I had to sort out my new life, which consisted of doctor visits, trips to the pharmacy, and the threat of unpleasant side effects.

Physical therapy helped me heal both physically and emotionally. I could have developed something called frozen shoulder from the surgery. I wasn't able to lift my arm over my head. My surgeon suggested exercises, but I needed more help. That's when I went to physical therapist Ethan White. His own mother had survived breast cancer, and he had a mission to help other women because of his mother's experience. He massaged this and that and explained that the sheath under the skin was damaged, but he could help me fix it and get my arm moving again. It was good to have direction and a plan to get stronger. Physical therapy visits were a real lift. I was not just stuck in this situation! I could do something about it and get better.

I was also secretly hoping Doug would not get the call to go to Europe this year. Every year for the past several years he traveled to Europe to do play-by-play for NFL Europe. It was a wonderful gig! He got paid to go to London, Barcelona, and Frankfurt. I got to tag along during those trips, and it was a dream come true. The best part of those trips was that Doug and I could go off on an excursion for a few days before the game. These trips allowed us as a couple to take time with each other and remember why we fell in love in the first place. But this year I probably wouldn't be able to go, I thought.

A dear friend urged me over the years to grab any opportunity to travel with my husband. She said that couples who were still married after more than thirty years always made it a point to travel, to take a little time together away from the kids. The thought of some time away sounded good. That's why I didn't want to pass up this wonderful opportunity to bond with my husband.

I had made up my own support group, choosing women I wanted to pattern myself after during my illness. One of those women was a teacher and neighbor. She'd had breast cancer more than a year before me. But she was spunky and positive and didn't let it ruin her life. Her friends marveled that she continued walking during her chemotherapy treatments. I wanted to be like her. So when I was panicked and sad at the thought that I might not be able to travel with Doug this year, I picked up the phone and called Helen Dickinson.

"Hello, Helen?" I said. "It's Brenda. Remember when you said to call if I needed anything? Well I'm feeling a little upset and confused. Doug is leaving to go to Europe and I want to go, but I'm worried I might be too sick to go."

Helen told me, "I traveled with my husband all throughout my chemotherapy. I was a little tired and had to rest more than I normally would, but I went anyway." Her words were like a chorus of angels from heaven. There was hope that I could go.

I quizzed my oncologist about the trip. He said if I wanted to go and felt up to it, I should go. I looked at the calendar and it looked as if the timing was good. The trip would be the third week after a chemo treatment. That's when I would start to feel better. The treatments were every three weeks and that third week I'd start to feel stronger just before the next one knocked me down again.

As the weeks progressed I got good news that was reason to celebrate. Dr. Cantrell said, "I've decided to reduce your chemo treatments from eight to four. New research has come out, and the last four treatments could prove more toxic to your system and not provide enough benefit. The taxol can cause neuropathy. Your hands or feet could go numb. If you take it, it would provide only a one percent benefit. It's like flipping a coin, but I think this is the right thing to do."

I was elated and petrified at the same time. I would only have one more chemo treatment. No more jabs in my arm, sliding that plastic into my vein. But did I want that extra one percent insurance that the cancer wouldn't return? Since my livelihood partly depended on my ability to type scripts, I was convinced we'd come to the right conclusion.

The plan was now clear. Three months after my surgery, I was heading to Frankfurt, Germany, to meet Doug. His parents offered to come up from Florida to watch the boys along with Nessa, our nanny. They would make a good team. They'd done it before and knew the routine.

I was concerned that I might catch an illness during the trip because of my weakened immune system. I asked if it was possible to get an anti-biotic just in case I got sick, and Dr. Cantrell obliged. That was a little bottle of insurance that I could make it through the trip.

Packing was a little different. Underwear—check. Reinforced post-surgical bras—check. Pants, skirts, and wigs. Check, check, check. Why did I take more than one wig? Well, you never know. If I lost one or singed one, I'd have another to replace it. It's easy to singe wigs. I ruined one of my favorite wigs just opening the oven while cooking dinner. I laughed to myself that the guys and gals x-raying my luggage might think I was a spy or double agent. Kind of romantic!

I decided on the long blond wig for the trip. This was the sexiest one I owned. The word *sexy* might sound funny coming from a woman who still had the second and third phase of her plastic surgery ahead. But we were a couple still in love and I wanted to look my best. I even packed all my special wig shampoos and de-tanglers.

## Healing Is a Choice

The day I boarded the plane I felt like a sixteen-year-old about to go on her first date. I had butterflies in my stomach, hoping Doug would enjoy this trip with me, even though I was not quite the same. I had a seat all the way in the back of the plane. I felt this was a good choice—at least most of the germs were ahead of me. I was seated next to a pleasant man with a receding hairline. Little did he know how much we had in common!

"Hi, I'm Joe." He gave me a friendly greeting. This was good, a nice person who could make the long flight much more pleasant. When I got settled in, I noticed he was dressed like a pilot. I joked, "Shouldn't you be sitting up in the front seat? You could see better up there to fly the plane."

"Sure," he laughed. "Actually I'm not the pilot for this flight. I fly planes for a private company in Saudi Arabia." I thought that was a fascinating, exciting job. We chatted about his job and much more. Joe mentioned he'd flown in Vietnam and talked about a comrade who'd lost an arm. He said, "I can't imagine anything worse than losing a part of your body. I don't think I could handle it. That image still haunts me."

This was my chance to minister to him. I'd asked God to use me. I said, "It's funny how people adapt. I know a little boy who has one arm. He was born with only one arm and he swims and plays baseball, basketball, and golf. In fact, he's stronger than any one child I know his age. He's a good friend of my son. He is going to grow up and do something special, because he overcomes every obstacle. You just don't know how something bad can reveal a blessing."

I wasn't ready to tell him that I'd lost a part of my body a few months ago. Then he said something that made me realize I wasn't delivering the message, I was receiving it. Joe said, "Yeah, I wish my girlfriend felt that way. She had breast cancer…"

The words stunned me. Was God working in His mysterious way?

"And it wasn't the cancer that broke us up; it was her attitude. I travel a lot, and after the operation she became very jealous and suspicious every time I went somewhere. I loved her so much and still would be with her if she hadn't accused me of things I didn't do. I just couldn't take it anymore. I stuck by her through the surgery and the chemo. But she wouldn't give me a break. She just accused me all the time of doing something wrong, of cheating on her. If she hadn't done that we'd still be together. I really loved her. It's unfortunate." He shook his head and looked down thoughtfully.

This man had no idea I was a breast cancer survivor. Was this a message God intended for me to hear? You betcha.

I remember learning about self-fulfilling prophecies in psychology class. People believe something and because they act as if their fears are true, the people around them do the very things they fear. Her bitterness drove him away. Her accusations put distance between them. I understood her pain. She was calling out to him for help. He didn't understand that. She wanted him simply to reassure her. But when he did, she wouldn't believe him. She wanted to believe he was faithful, but the scars of the cancer and surgery wouldn't allow her to heal emotionally.

I decided right then and there; healing on the inside is a choice. Cancer puts a forked road in your path. You can choose to allow it to make you bitter, which is the easy choice…or you can choose to allow it to make you better spiritually. God spoke to me through this man's tragic story of a lost love. I could tell he loved her deeply, but because she would not allow that emotional healing to happen, the couple split up.

I thought about Doug and his trips away from home. I would choose to trust him and choose to put that part of my life in God's hands. Doug had always been faithful. He was a part of me. I would not let myself sink into self-pity and jealousy. I never told Joe I was a breast cancer survivor as well. I didn't want to make him feel bad about anything he'd said. Everything he said was such a blessing. It opened my eyes.

## Second Honeymoon

Was the trip the second honeymoon I'd hoped for? It was better than I'd imagined. While Doug worked I did something wild and crazy, something I felt guilty about at home…I slept. I snuggled under the covers in the middle of the day, pulled a good book out and read, then nodded off. I'd been pushing so hard during the chemotherapy to live my normal life that I'd completely exhausted myself. This was a gift, time to rest, while Doug was happy working at his dream job.

When the day came for us to travel on our own for a few days, we decided to take an easier sightseeing tour than we had in past years. Instead of hopping from country to country by airplane, we would rent a car instead and explore Germany's famous Black Forest.

My favorite stop was a small quaint town called Baden-Baden. Our hotel was highly recommended by the travel journal. It was perfect. We were planning to go to a romantic dinner later. After showering, putting my wig in place, and styling it as best I could, I thought I'd lay down for just a minute.

About an hour or so later, I woke up to see Doug watching some sort of German sports channel. He couldn't understand a word that was being said, but it was still sports. It passed the time while his exciting wife snored through the dinner hour. The aftereffects of chemo and a little sightseeing and swimming were more than my body could handle. I really could have easily skipped dinner and slept all night. But that wasn't the plan.

We strolled through the cobblestone streets of Baden-Baden, window-shopped, talked, and laughed. We found a cute little German restaurant that had a roaring fire going. It was perfect! The dinner was delicious. I thought, *This is one of life's most wonderful moments.* Then we came back to the hotel room and the bed called to me. It was time to rest again.

I was as happy as a clam. I walked into the bathroom, locked the door (which was my new ritual since my surgery), and shed my clothes to change for bed. I looked in the mirror as I took off my wig, and the tears started to flow. I figured it was part of the aftershock. I think it was like releasing a pressure valve. At home, I worked so hard to be strong that I didn't give myself time to grieve for my losses and accept the new me. This time alone gave me that chance to let the cancer experience to settle in, so that I could put it where it now belonged...behind me. That was one of the last good cries I had about having cancer. It marked the end of feeling like the victim. It was time to start living again. I prayed to God, *I'm giving this to You to handle, because I can't worry about it any more...I'm done with it.* I'd been molded and pruned. It was out with the old and in with what was new and vibrant.

## I've Been Pruned

One Sunday morning, almost a year after my surgery, the Bible lesson in church was about how God prunes away what is useless. I had been pruned in many ways in the last year. The Gospel of John says it this way:

> *"I am the true vine, and my Father is the gardener. He cuts off every branch in me that bears no fruit, while every branch that does bear fruit he prunes so that it will be even more fruitful....No branch can bear fruit by itself; it must remain in the vine. Neither can you bear fruit unless you remain in me. I am the vine; you are the branches. If a man remains in me and I in him, he will bear much fruit; apart from me you can do nothing." —John 15:1–5*

That Sunday morning in class, we were having a good discussion about that Scripture. I wanted to shout, I've been pruned! But just as I got ready to share my thoughts, class was dismissed. So I'll share with you now how I've been pruned.

Before I had cancer, things like hair, make-up, furniture, new clothes, and sending my kids to the right summer camps were extremely important to me. But now those things take a back seat to the really important things in life—things like spending time with my friends and family, talking with someone who's just been diagnosed with cancer, or taking care of myself by resting or running. I realize there's a wealth of information in the Bible. I like to discover verses that apply to my life. I take time to appreciate the incredible world the Lord made. Fussing over the little things in life like traffic jams or a burnt dinner just doesn't seem worth it anymore. I look for the good and embrace it. There is so much good in our world.

Now, my favorite thing is to listen to my children. Things like, "Mommy, if this is a free country, why isn't everything free? Why do we have to pay for groceries?" Or this one made me chuckle: "Mommy, how did you get those colored marshmallows to be hard and to taste like mint?"

"Honey, those are mints, not marshmallows," I answered.

Yes, cancer has been a life-changing experience. Just imagine your former rivals and competitors becoming like sisters and brothers instantly. Two people I had competed with over the years and prayed for, because I thought they would just as soon throw me in the lake as look at me, came to me and embraced me with their love and support. God really is good.

But most of all, it mended a bridge in my own family, one that I had been praying about for months before I was diagnosed...it reunited my two sisters. Linda and Susan have an oil and water kind of relationship. The rift between them had happened months earlier, and they had hardly spoken. But while Linda was in town helping to care for me, she and Susan talked on the phone.

I had just made one of my valiant attempts to make it a few feet from my bed to the bathroom all on my own. While sitting there, I saw bugs climbing the walls but I knew it was the morphine and not real. I saw smoke climbing the walls as well. The morphine was doing its job on the pain, anyway, for the most part.

Still pondering the smoke and bugs, I heard the phone ring. My sister Linda answered. "Hello? Uh, she's in the bathroom right now. Oh," she said. "Well this is Linda...Okay, I'll tell her you called." And that was it...the bottle of oil and water had been shaken up during this storm, even if just a little bit. They talked and that was good.

Before cancer, these were things that I was always too busy to do. But now I had time, and plenty of it. Linda also helped me go through the hundreds of cards and letters that poured in. We were both overwhelmed by the love and support from so many people. I told her I lived in a great community where the people were so caring. Card after card read, *We're praying for you, get well soon.* These cards and letters were like God speaking through so many. They were encouraging and uplifting. With all those prayers, I knew I'd have to get up out of this bed and be Brenda again.

A few days after I returned home and was resting in bed, the phone rang. It was my surgeon, Dr. Susan Winchester. I was very impressed that a busy surgeon would take the time to call.

"How are you?" she asked.

"Oh, I'm fine, thanks." I responded as if it was any other day.

"No, how are you really doing? How's the depression?" she asked.

"The depression?" I asked.

She went on to explain that depression was a part of the after-surgery healing process many women experience.

I said, "No, I'm not really depressed, but I'll work on it."

After we hung up, I thought about it. I realized there had been those moments. While I was heavily drugged on the pain medicine, I thought, *What will people think of me now? Will my husband still love me? Can I go on? Will I ever be Mommy again?* Was it depressing dealing with the after effects of surgery? Was it depressing that I knew I'd have to undergo chemotherapy and lose my hair because cancer had invaded two lymph nodes? Yes. Did I cry? You betcha! In fact, crying, I was told by Dr. Susan Winchester, is great for healing and for the immune system. So cry; it's okay. It was a part of my healing process.

I felt like a child holding onto the Lord's hand. He led me through every step of the way. I kept thinking about Proverbs 3:5: "Trust in the Lord with all your heart and lean not on your own under-standing." I knew God had a plan for me, and I was going to abide by that plan wherever it led me.

## Back to Work

Within three weeks and a few days, I was back at work. I was proud of that because I had been told it might take longer to recuperate. But I knew it was time to head back to work on one particular morn-ing. All three boys were running toward me. I thought to myself, *Oh, aren't they cute, they all want to hug their momma.* Though I still had pain in my chest, I thought, *I'll give them the best hug I can.*

Then I heard it and wanted to scream and run. My oldest said, "Mom's base and you're it!" I had apparently been sitting around the house too long. My children had put me in the same category with the tree used for a game of tag.

My next move was to call my boss at work. "Hello, Garry? Yes, this is Brenda. I'm doing great, but can I come back to work? I think it's safer there." I chuckled and I told him the tag story.

I remember walking back into the newsroom for the first time since I'd had surgery. As Doug escorted me into the building, I felt nervous. How would people react? I got my answer quickly when the assignment editor Dave Perry saw me, stood up, and applauded, and was followed by my other co-workers. Tears filled my eyes and I knew I'd be okay and life at work would go on as well.

## Fight the Disease

I found another way to feel better and not bitter was to focus on how to fight the disease and not be defeated by it. I kept a close watch on the news wires to find the latest in research to pass along to other cancer patients to give them hope.

There is so much research that is promising. Some of the information crossing the wire reminded me of my mother's advice. Eat your fruit and vegetables. Get plenty of rest. Exercise and avoid stress. One study found that women who worked at night had a higher incidence of breast cancer. They believed it had something to do with the body clock and bright light at night when the body was supposed to be resting. All this was thought to raise hormone levels, which could cause cancer to grow. Other studies that I embraced were that water, melon, and chocolate were great antioxidants. I could handle those cancer-fighting foods. A study showed that aspirin blocked the growth of cancer. I can see my oncologist saying, "Take two aspirins and call me in the morning."

I found knowledge was empowering. It made me feel better to know more about the disease I was doing battle with. The more information the better. I wanted to empower others as well.

*Chapter Six*

# Are You Going to Hurt Brenda Today? A Protective Husband

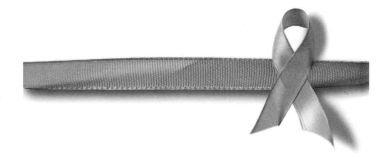

*T*he worst part of the chemo was the pokes in the arm. Doug had been my bodyguard through the surgery, recovery, and now through the chemotherapy. He drove me to my treatments because the drugs they gave me for the nausea would knock me for a loop. During each treatment he would walk me into the room where the nurse would put the PICC (peripherally inserted central venous catheter) line into my arm—a tube they would plug the chemo into. The needle and tube would have to be placed just right. I was not blessed with big veins, so this always presented a challenge for the nurse to find just the right vein to invade.

On one particular treatment day, I felt the worst pain of all during this process. The nurse couldn't find a vein that worked, so she had to "go shopping for one," as she put it. That meant poke after poke after poke. I had to get up and go to the bathroom to splash cold water on my face. I felt faint and nauseated by the pain. While I was in there, Doug, my dear, sweet husband, who stands about six feet four inches tall, was talking to my nurse. He said, "You aren't going to hurt Brenda any more, are you?" Even though the bathroom door was closed, I could see him towering over the petite woman. He wasn't threatening, just trying to strongly encourage her to get it done with the least amount of pain possible. He can be like such a guard dog when it comes to his family. It is an admirable trait. I smiled at the thought that he loved me so much that he would do anything to protect me.

This big, strong man who cringed and turned away if he saw a stranger get a shot in the arm on TV shows or news reports stood by me during each poke. He winced with me. We weren't just two people in that room. We were like one. I opened the door and smiled at my knight in shining armor.

"You aren't scaring the nurses, are you honey?" I asked.

He gave me his sheepish smile.

Then the nurse smiled and said, "Let's get this over with." I wasn't sure if she would punish me for bringing my bodyguard or get the vein on the next poke. I said the Lord's Prayer silently to myself. And it's a funny thing…she found the right vein. The poking was over. And I have to mention that at the next chemotherapy session, she got the vein on the first try then, too.

Whenever Doug was near me during the recovery from surgery or the chemotherapy, I felt better. I felt complete. His support and encouragement meant so much. I knew he was going through so much inside as well. He also went with me to "Touching You," a wig shop and salon for women with cancer. I went there after the surgery to buy some specially-designed supportive bras for mastectomy patients who have had reconstruction. I had to be measured. I wasn't really sure what size Dr. Beckenstein had provided me with.

I was whisked away to a private room while Doug sat in the waiting area and flipped through magazines. Carol Cauthen, the owner of the shop, was also a breast cancer survivor. She shared her own experience with me. In fact, I remembered she had come to visit me in the hospital while I was tripping on morphine shortly after surgery. Her story inspired me. She told me how she continued working through the chemotherapy. She counseled me about the hair loss. She even cried with me. She said this business was her way of giving back. I felt very safe while in her company. If she could survive and go on to have a son against the odds given by her doctors, then I could beat this thing, too!

As Doug and I were leaving, he said, "I didn't know Olivia Newton-John had breast cancer." I said, "I didn't realize that either." He went on to say that Peggy Fleming had it and mentioned several other famous women had also had it. He'd been reading a copy of an old "People" magazine that featured famous breast cancer survivors. Just knowing that those strong, beautiful women had it, dealt with it, and survived was a comfort.

## Dealing with Anger

Doug was constantly coming home with stories of hope and survival. He saw me at my worst and lowest points after surgery. He saw me cry and held me in his arms to comfort me. When I asked if he could still love me, he reassured me. God sent this man to be my partner. At times I needed to be there for him…and now I needed him to be there for me. He said all the right things the week after surgery. I felt like I was in shock for weeks, but then there was the next emotion to deal with—anger. I never got angry at God, but I did have unexplained anger at times. Little things would bring feelings of rage. If I dropped something, it might make me really mad. I later realized I wasn't mad at that particular event. I figured out that this was part of the healing process. I would get mad about something so insignificant that it would make me shake my own head at myself.

For example, after I had returned to work and tried to get life back to normal, I was left out of the planning for a school party. I logically knew that I'd been out of the loop because of my illness. People probably thought I was too weak to help. They were being thoughtful. But I was ready to reclaim my role as Mommy. I was angry over nothing.

While I took my daily walk, I felt anger well up inside me. I had no particular reason to feel that way, but it was there. I knew I was angry that I had cancer. I wasn't angry at anyone. I was just angry. Walking and praying and talking helped. I consulted with my friend Lisa Baggett about the anger. She had been a counselor and told me it was normal. Her son had had a benign brain tumor, and for a long time after that crisis she felt pangs of anger that he had to get sick. Even when the surgery to remove the tumor was a success, she had to deal with that emotion.

I told Doug that I knew I was overreacting to some things but that it had something to do with the emotions of a cancer diagnosis. He always understood. I finally asked the Lord to take the anger away. I had no room in my life for it. After all, I was trying to enjoy every day. Doug supported me through that time when I was an argument waiting to happen. He was patient and kind. He didn't always understand why I was upset. He just knew I was working through the process of coming to grips with the fact that I had cancer. Sometimes even the things he said to try to help would lead me to tears. I wanted him to fix everything for me. But through the tears I came to a wonderful revelation. Jesus is perfect, but the rest of us sometimes say and do the wrong things. That's okay; we are human. But with the Lord's guidance, we can stay on track.

## Taking a Moment

At first after the diagnosis, Doug would urge me not

to cry. He wanted me to be happy and strong. But as Dr. Winchester reminded him, crying is good for the immune system. After that, he'd look at me and say, "Is this one of those moments?" I'd say, "Yes, honey, I'm having a moment." The word *moment* spoke volumes in our home. It meant this was a time I needed for myself to cry and deal with what was happening in my life. "Yes, I just need one right now," I'd say. Then he'd hug me. I knew he wanted to make it all go away. He wanted to make it all better. I wanted him to make it go away, too, but I knew he couldn't. The only thing he could do for me was to allow me to have that "moment" and stand by me and let me know he was there.

I can also tell you there was plenty of laughter. Sometimes what was happening to me seemed so ridiculous, Doug and I would just break down and laugh. That too became a great way to release tension. He'd call me "baldy." I'd lightly slap him and we'd both laugh. The chiding was welcomed. I knew if he was kidding me, I must really be okay. My doctor also encouraged laughter; it's good for the immune system, just as tears are.

Bald jokes ran rampant in our house. I really had fun with Doug when I tried to turn the tables and pretended to find a bald spot on the top of his head. I never saw a man go running for a hand-held mirror so fast in my life! He wasn't really going bald, but for a brief second he understood how I felt. Being able to laugh at myself and the whole situation really helped.

I know Doug went through a lot of emotional changes. But even though he had turmoil inside, he always tried to remain calm and be my strong rock of Gibraltar. I hope his story, included at the end of the book, will help other men going through the same thing not to feel so alone.

# Chapter Seven

# *Running From Cancer and Running to God*

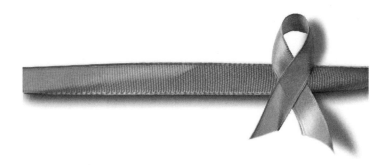

My eyes were still shut when I heard the familiar call: "Dada...Mama...ball." Our 20-month-old was awake. As had become the ritual since my operation, "Dada" plucked him out of his crib, changed him, and put him in the high chair. The other two boys started shuffling around, and after a quick hug—"good morning Mom, good morning Dad"—they were off to catch 30 minutes of cartoons before breakfast. While the cat was

chasing the mouse on TV and Doug started breakfast (also a ritual since my operation), I was getting
ready to hopefully defy the odds. I would rise from
my bed, throw on some shorts and a t-shirt, socks
and sneakers...oh yeah, and my flattering hat-hair
wig—a ball cap with nylon strands of hair velcroed
to its sides. I kissed my men goodbye. "I'll see ya in
40 minutes, honey," I said as I ventured outside to
be jumped on by our two-year-old beagle mix
named Copper.

My legs were bruised because of his jumping,
and because chemotherapy has left me a little more
fragile. It takes bruises a little longer to heal now.
"It's time to run, boy," I said. As we crossed the
wooden bridge over the creek, I noticed it was a
cool morning, thanks to the rain the night before.
My morning ritual would have to be pumped up
today. You see, the day before my oncologist had
prescribed tamoxifen, a five-year cancer drug that
would beat down the cancer but could also sap my
strength, cause me to gain weight, and cause hot
flashes. As a woman who had lost both breasts, her
hair, eyelashes, and eyebrows, I was going to fight
to keep the trim figure so expertly provided by my
plastic surgeon.

While I embraced the cancer-fighting qualities
of tamoxifen, I also planned to do battle with the

side effects by eating well and getting plenty of exercise. It made me a little mad to think, *After all I'd been through, now I have to battle weight gain?!* But I could use this anger to get a good run in, followed by a short walk. I heard the pounding of hammers up near the lake—workers were building a new dock for parents and children to use for fishing. The strike of the hammers was like listening to a battalion marching out of step. And while the hammers pounded, my feet pounded the pavement of the cart path on the golf course behind our home. After 15 minutes of running, my heart began to join my feet and the hammers in the pounding sonata. The endorphins were kicking in, and I thought, *Take that, tamoxifen.* This was a great morning. In fact, I was reminded by the sound of birds singing that, yes, every day we are alive is a great day, because it is a gift from God. We can rise above the afflictions, the side effects, and any setbacks with the help of God.

As I ran, I remembered the Bible verses many people sent my way to encourage me through the cancer crisis. I thought about God's word in Isaiah promising His protection through difficulties:

*"When you pass through the waters, I will be with you; and when you pass through the*

*rivers, they will not sweep over you. When you walk through the fire, you will not be burned; the flames will not set you ablaze. For I am the Lord, your God, the Holy One of Israel, your Savior."* —Isaiah 43:2–3

## Running from Cancer

While pounding the pavement and watching my beagle chase a squirrel and bark his sort of gurgled howl, I prayed, *Please Lord, don't let this drug rob me of the joy You want for us in life. Let the drug do its job without affecting my moods or hurting my body. Thank You, Lord, for this day and every other that You give me as a gift.* I looked at my watch and realized I had run farther than I had in the last several months. I ran for a solid 20 minutes. I kept running, hoping my watch would show that I had put in another five minutes. It seemed like the hands of the watch had frozen, but it was just my fatigue. It really was time to walk.

That morning I gained a bit of a victory by running farther even on tamoxifen. Life goes on. As we walked back toward the house I noticed the sun glistening on a snaking creek that ran along the golf course. I thought how much that creek was like life. It always has twists and turns and has to keep moving. Sometimes you don't know what you'll find around the bend. But with God's hand involved, you can bet He will turn whatever lies ahead into a blessing. That is exactly what God allowed to result from the cancer. I got a chance to savor life, family, and friends. I now listen to the birds in the morning and thank God every day that I'm alive.

As the weeks passed, I increased my running time from twenty minutes to thirty, then to forty-five minutes a day. My next goal was to run an hour, then and hour and a half. Every week I'd increase my time by five minutes. At first, how far I ran didn't seem to matter.

I didn't start running because I heard about Lance Armstrong, but after running for my own health, hearing about his third consecutive win of the Tour de France certainly inspired me to keep running. After all, isn't that the hardest part of any exercise regimen, sticking to it? Armstrong won the Tour de France after he had battled testicular cancer and brain and lung tumors. Hearing about Armstrong's endurance and tenacity, I understood all too well that a little competition in an international bike race was nothing compared with battling cancer.

There are no wimps in cancer centers. Facing the possibility of death, the loss of breasts, and the many kinds of pain one experiences, I learned that the challenge of a morning run is nothing. Running has replaced my morning cup of coffee. Before cancer, I drank two to three extra large cups every morning. Often in the afternoon I'd have another cup, then at about nine pm, before the evening news, I'd guzzle one more to pump me up before the ten o'clock news. Now as part of my new healthy regimen, I've given up the black stuff.

Instead, I run.

## Running to God

Almost nine weeks after my last chemo treatment, my husband and I packed up our three boys and went to the beach. While at the beach we did all the beachy things: swam, built sandcastles, jumped in the waves, and ate seafood. I continued to run about 30–40 minutes a day. While we were searching for a dinner spot to feed our hungry brood, we cruised the strip on the beach. I asked my husband Doug how far the grocery store was. He said, "It's a mile."

I was shocked. I'd been running farther and faster than I'd thought. I asked him to drive down to the three-mile mark down on the road that runs along the beach. I'd never run six miles at one time in my life! The next morning I looked for the three-mile mark down the beach road and made it there.

On the way there, I prayed and thanked God for the beautiful day, and for being alive to enjoy this day with my family. I prayed to keep the cancer away and to heal other cancer victims. I prayed for an hour, just talking to God. While I ran, I couldn't believe how good I felt and that I was closing in on my goal of three miles. I made it! After I ran three miles back, I would have run six miles for the first time in my life. Not even the flattened turtles kept me from turning around.

I used to dread running; it was a chore. Now I thought what a privilege it was to be able to run. I used to run with a walkman so the music would keep me going. But now my time with God sets my feet in motion.

My heart was pounding when I rounded the last corner to head back to the condominium. I thought as I ran how we often underestimate ourselves. I felt that God wanted me to tell others that they can do more. They can run that extra mile or take on that extra project at church, because with His help all things are possible. But only if it's God's will, not your own.

Three weeks later, I was visiting with my friend Lisa Baggett. She was confused about some life choices she was making. She wanted to go back to school, but wasn't sure about it. I remembered my run at the beach that morning. I said, "I believe God can help us do anything and that we often underestimate ourselves." How many times have you thought, *I can't do that; I'm not smart enough or good enough?* None of us are good enough. But God often chooses the least likely person to do His work.

I came from a steel town in Pennsylvania, where many people grew up and worked in the mill. Women became secretaries, teachers, or nurses. I knew I wasn't organized enough to be a secretary or teacher and was too squeamish to become a nurse. I remember my father telling me those were my options. But God had a different plan for this little girl from Coatesville, Pennsylvania. He molded me into a news anchor. God had a plan for my life, and I held on for the ride!

I never intended to be a news anchor. I had intended to go into advertising and retire by the time I turned thirty. Ha! That was my plan. But as usual, God had a better plan. While I was in college, doors to broadcasting kept opening and doors to advertising kept closing. I got one of two spots as an anchor for the school magazine program, I got a morning radio gig, and I interned at local stations and landed a job at TV-28. I read the news on this family-owned and operated station every hour on the hour. I felt God wanted me in broadcasting; I just never understood why He blessed me so much. I felt I was never doing enough for Him. But now, I hope God will use me as a vehicle for His message, and the thought of that is exhilarating.

## Troubles Lead to Blessings

While running back home in the neighborhood and praying as I usually do, I was going up a hill. I started to wish I lived in a flat place like Florida, where the hills were non-existent. But then I realized I needed to thank God for the hills and mountains I run into during the marathon of life. Think about it—when you are hit with a challenge and you have to run uphill, you know pretty soon you'll get to run downhill for a while.

The hills also remind me that life's troubles can lead to our greatest blessings. This astounding realization came as I ran up and down a hill and thought how all my worst disasters led to my greatest blessings. Losing a job led to me meeting my husband. A difficult pregnancy gave me time to grow closer to God.

Cancer, too, has led to so many blessings I can't count them all. Probably the most important is my appreciation for life. I used to dread exercise. Now it's such a privilege. I think every morning when I run, *I could be in a hospital bed. But I'm not! I'm out here with the birds and trees and I'm running. Thank You, God.*

One Saturday morning after I made it up the first steep incline (and in Birmingham there are many), I was enjoying the downhill trek when I realized something. We all have problems. It's not the problems that matter; it's how we deal with them. We can be defeated by a crisis or we can get up and fight and look for the good beyond it.

Can you think of the worst thing that happened but which led to our greatest blessing? Jesus was crucified on a cross. That was the punishment for murderers and common criminals. He didn't deserve that. But it's that crisis that led to our salvation. It led to the greatest blessing the world has ever seen—the resurrection of Christ! So the next time you run uphill against the wind, remember it's leading you to something better. Thank God for the hard times, because they are molding us, shaping us, drawing us closer to Him. After you get up that hill, remember it's a lot easier on the way down.

## The 10K, At My Pace

As the weeks and months passed, running provided me with quiet time to pray. My distance increased, and some friends at work invited me to run in the Birmingham Mercedes Marathon, a half marathon or full marathon, as part of a fundraiser to help fight cancer. How could I refuse? I was in the battle up to my elbows. I wanted to defeat this killer. If running 26.2 miles would help, count me in! I started training with the Team In Training group, which raises money for the Leukemia and Lymphoma Society. I would be running for Shelby, a little girl with leukemia.

I ran seven miles for the first time in my life with that group. We met early in the morning, at the crack of dawn. In October, those mornings are quite brisk, but we pop on our hats and gloves and brave the cold. After all, we're only cold for about a half-mile or so. My husband started running longer distances and said he would join me in the marathon. "Hey, want to run in the Vulcan Run 10K? It'll be a good warm-up for the marathon," he said. Again, how could I refuse?

On a cold morning in November, the Vulcan Run began in downtown Birmingham near the entrance to the Tutwiler Hotel, a historic hotel in Birmingham. It was my first 10K race. I started out okay, but it quickly became evident that I was out of my league. People flowed around me like a raging river. I watched a four-year-old pass me, running with his dad. A man running with a limp passed me, then a trotting dog, a heavy-set woman, and a man who appeared to be about 90. I was humiliated at first, but then I came to a wonderful realization.

We all have our own pace. It doesn't really matter if you're fast or slow. Your pace is your pace. There will always be people stronger and weaker than you are. God accepts us the way we are and loves us as individuals. We should be proud of our pace, no matter if it's in a race or in our daily lives. You have to live at your own pace. Sometimes cancer and the treatment will cause your pace to slow down, and that's okay. That slower pace can allow you to smell the roses and realize what's really important in life. So run your race at your own pace and don't get frustrated because you can't keep up with the four-year-old running ahead of you. Enjoy the journey you're on and realize you're not running the race by yourself. God is always there right next to you when you need help.

As the months passed, I continued training for the Mercedes Marathon. Once a week the group of Team In Training runners would meet to run. It was a thrill to run with so many elite runners. At six thirty on Sunday mornings we'd run in rain, sleet, or snow. Even the darkness before dawn didn't stop us during the winter months. We ran 6 miles, 7 miles,

9 miles, then 13, 15, and 20! Never in my life did I dream I'd be able to run 20 miles.

> *"Jesus looked at them and said, "With man this is impossible, but with God all things are possible."* —Matthew 19:26

The Team In Training coaches taught me how to gradually increase my mileage so I could reach my goal. During one of the first runs I was glad to see fellow breast cancer survivor Stacy Gordon. We became running buddies on Sunday mornings. Stacy was also a tri-athlete and continued to compete in races and triathlons while she was undergoing chemotherapy. Her story had inspired me while I was undergoing physical therapy. Because of Stacey, I knew I could continue to exercise through chemo.

A week before the marathon, I did a news story about Les Longshore, a 76-year-old marathon runner. Les started running in his fifties. He'd run more than 30 marathons and logged 45,000 miles. He was so inspiring. He told me it was more important for people of his age to run or walk because if they didn't, they'd just stop moving altogether. He was agile, in shape, and had a sharp mind—all things he attributed to his physical fitness. As I interviewed him on that cold February morning, I thought *He has found peace in this sport.*

How often we tell ourselves we can't when we can! What a gift life is, and what a gift our bodies are. God gave us the tools to keep us healthy. He provided us with fresh fruits and vegetables, many of which are packed with cancer-fighting elements. My favorite cancer fighting foods are watermelon, packed with a cancer-fighter called licopene, spaghetti sauce, and chocolate. These are anti-oxidants and can help prevent cancer and heart disease. Some researchers and cancer patients believe diet can help fend off cancer and help the body fight it.

While training for the marathon, I ate plenty of vegetables. My veggie of choice was spinach. True story: before my second baby, I couldn't look at spinach, much less eat the stuff. But it's funny how things change; now it's a real treat for me. My new healthier way of eating was making a difference in my endurance. My body actually had some good fuel to work with.

## Running the Marathon

The night before the marathon, I was scared! I asked myself, "Are you crazy? What have you gone and done now?" I thought, *I can't run a marathon.*

Then I thought, *No, I can't run it alone.* But I knew I wouldn't be alone. God would be with me. I actually slept peacefully that night after praying about it.

The alarm went off in the dark at about 4:15 am. Since the marathon started at 7:00 am, we had just enough time to get dressed, parked, and stretched before the race.

When we arrived in downtown Birmingham, we saw runners everywhere. Some were dressed in warm running outfits, others just had shorts and t-shirts on. Many were warming up by jogging up and down the street. No warm up for me, I'd need every ounce of energy for the race. It was nice to see other runners I knew, from the health club or from our Sunday morning runs. Doug and I, along with my friend Kori Rooney, stretched and talked about what a great morning it was. I looked at my watch. It was just before 7:00 am. Time to line up.

There was a sea of runners. Doug was beside me. My heart pounded with excitement. On this day I wasn't just running a race, I was running a marathon. I wasn't just running for myself, I was running for cancer patients. First the horn sounded and the wheelchair participants took off. A few minutes later the next horn sounded and we were off! The sound of thousands of running shoes hitting the pavement was an incredible sound. It was almost like hearing the sound of a heavy rain. We rounded past the civic center, and Doug was keeping a faster pace than my 11-minute mile, but I felt good. I was concerned that if I started out too fast I'd have nothing left for the end of the race. But I was glad he was there. We were a team.

Running through Birmingham is very different than driving through. As we passed the Sixteenth Street Baptist Church, I reflected on the struggle those church members had in the early '60s and the horror of the bomb that killed those four little girls. While the church was a reminder of Birmingham's past, we also wound around the streets of Birmingham and passed the McWane Center, which represented the city's present and future. This science center was a favorite stop for my children and many other children. The operators took textbook science lessons and turned them into children's play. Then we passed the Alabama Theatre, a restored movie theatre run by a man named Cecil Whitmier. My in-laws have fond memories of dating there during the 1950s.

During the run, I prayed as I usually do during runs. I thanked God for this perfect day and asked Him to use me. I thought about an e-mail I'd received the week before the race. It read: "I want you to know you saved my life. I am married and have a seven-year-old son. I've had colon cancer twice and have constant pain and sickness from chemo. I was going to commit suicide, but hearing your story gave me hope. You showed me there is light at the end of the tunnel. I am unemployed and only able to supply the basics to my family. But I see God in your smile, and I want to live now." I thought, *That is why I'm running.*

I had asked two of the station's photographers, Bill Castle and Stephanie Brooks, to help document the race. I wanted to show what it was like for a novice to run a marathon for the first time. These two good friends ran their own marathons that day. As I ran the course, I'd see Stephanie or Bill along the way as they shot some film of me running. Bill ran a lot of the way with a 35-pound camera on his shoulder. He and Stephanie helped file a story about the marathon, which aired during the 6pm news.

When I crossed the finish line, I wanted to cry. I thanked God. I thought, *This is for Shelby, the little girl with leukemia, and for cancer patients everywhere!* I couldn't believe I was actually crossing the finish line after running 26.2 miles. This was truly God's work, not mine.

Doug, my teammate through cancer, in life, and during this race, had finished ahead of me and was waiting for me at the end of my race. Coming home, we also felt victorious. We could tell our children, "Hey kids, Mommy and Daddy ran 26.2 miles!"

But my oldest son was mostly concerned that I might have come in last. He looked very relieved when I told him I did not. I told him I had even passed some big, strong men along the way. He smiled, and I knew somehow he realized that Mommy was okay and not weak from the cancer anymore!

# Chapter Eight

# *Helping Your Children Deal With Breast Cancer*

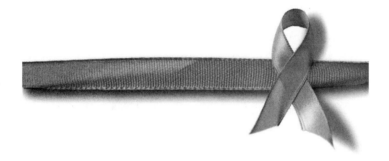

*I* not only pray for those who have cancer, I also pray for their children. After I spoke to a group of teachers, a pretty brunette came up to me, hugged me, and thanked me. She started to cry and told me that when she was a child, she had lost her mother to breast cancer. Many of the things I talked about brought back memories for her—things like the hair loss. I wanted to wipe away her tears and her pain and tell her something that would heal her.

But I knew all I could say was, "I'm so sorry." I wonder what scars my children will have from this cancer experience. I hope they'll be stronger and more understanding as a result.

The week before the surgery, I tried to comfort my children and find just the right Scriptures and words to ease the blow of Mommy going to the hospital...but the children ended up helping me.

## God's Arms Wrapped Around Us

One of the things I told my sons before I went into the hospital was that if they ever felt scared or lonely, they should just remember that God has His arms wrapped around them. I wanted them to have a source of comfort when I couldn't be there, and I knew that God loved them even more than I did. My boys listened gravely, but didn't respond.

After the surgery, when I was home but too weak to leave the bed, my sweet boy Gabby came into the bedroom. He crawled into bed beside me and lay there stiff and still like a toy soldier. There were several moments of silence, which is unusual for Gabby. I imagined he must have been pretty scared by a mommy who looked so weak. I could tell he was trying not to hurt me by moving the bed. But on this day, with his mom looking so frail, my little guy was reserved. Finally, after lying there quiet for about twenty minutes, out of the mouth of this babe came something I needed to hear.

He said, "Mommy, I feel God's arms around us right now!"

He'd been listening to the speech I made just a few days before the surgery. I had wondered at the time how much he understood. Those words came back to inspire me during what threatened to be a dark time filled with doubts about the future.

A few days after the diagnosis, Brooks was sitting on the sofa in the den. He was reading a book. Not just any book—it was his Bible.

"Whatcha reading, buddy?" I asked.

"It's about angels, Mom," he said very seriously. "Do they really help you in a car?" he asked.

"Let me see; angels help you when God asks them to. He knows when you need extra help." He showed me the sidebar story in his Kids Quest Bible, which read: *God watches over us. He uses angels to help us. If God wants an angel to be with us in the car, that is where the angel will be. If God wants the angel to be outside the car while it is moving, that is where the angel will be. Angels go wherever God tells them to go.*

I felt a sense of peace after sitting next to my seven-year-old son. Had God used this child to deliver His message? I knew He did! Psalm 121:1–5 says:

> *"I lift up my eyes to the hills—where does my help come from? My help comes from the Lord, the Maker of heaven and earth. He will not let your foot slip—he who watches over you will not slumber; indeed, he who watches over Israel will neither slumber nor sleep. The Lord watches over you."*

## Being Honest About Death

It was just four days before Christmas, and Doug, the boys, and I were driving down Highway 119. We passed a number of big beautiful homes that looked like estates. Finally, we passed a beautiful, enormous funeral home. It's the place I would want for my service. I heard the kids oohing and ahhing. Brooks said, "I want to live there."

Doug and I chuckled and looked at each other. "Honey," I said to Brooks, "that's a funeral home. It's a place people go to say goodbye to someone who's died. Friends and family gather to celebrate their life."

"They celebrate 'cause they died?" he asked.

"No," I said, "they celebrate their life."

I took this opportunity to try in a small way to prepare the children for a death in the family. Cancer forces you to face such things. I chuckle at how immature I had been just a year earlier when my son's two goldfish died. These were fish Brooks had gotten as part of his goody bag at a birthday party. *What kind of people force fish on you,* I thought, as I smiled and told Brooks to say thank you. The tiny goldfish came with a tiny bowl.

The pet store rep advised me that if I wanted to keep my fish alive, I'd need a bigger tank, with a filter. Wasn't this a form of extortion? "Buy the fish stuff or Goldy there will die." Trying to be a good mother and shield my son from the painful experience of a dead fish, I bought it all, hook, line, and sinker! Even though I did everything Mr. Pet Store advised, the fish died anyway. Instead of using the event as a lesson in life and death, I tried to shield my son from the terrible news. "Honey," I said, "I know you're wondering where Charlie and Swimmer went…well, they went to visit a relative fish. They travel through the pipes, you know." The story was getting more outrageous, and I began to sweat. I was digging myself in very deep.

"How do they travel through the pipes, Mommy? Can I go too?" I had gone too far; this wasn't being honest and I knew it.

When I shared the story with my co-anchor Josh Thomas, he said, "You're not doing them any favors. They need to know what's real." He was right. If I had it to do all over again, I would have just told him the truth. Kids are smarter than many adults, including me, give them credit for. In an effort to protect our children, we often miss the opportunity to teach. God gave us these little lives to help mold them.

I'm convinced that honesty helps children deal with cancer much better.

After returning to work following my surgery, a pretty blue-eyed, blond lady named Wanda McKoy came by the station to talk about the Komen Breast Cancer Foundation. She shared with me that her mother passed away from breast cancer.

She said, "I wish at age eleven they'd been honest with me. I remember pitching a fit while my mother tried to wash my hair. If I'd only known she was that sick, I wouldn't have done it." Years later, this sweet woman still felt the regret of an eleven-year-old. It's okay to be honest with children. Don't scare them unnecessarily...but be truthful.

My neighbor and good friend Kathy Mardis lost her mother to breast cancer when Kathy was a child. Now that she's grown with children of her own, she wishes she knew more about her mother's illness. Decades after her mother's death, she asked her aunt to fill her in on that part of her family history. It was like a book with a blank chapter in her life that needed to be filled in. She also told me, "I wish people would have talked about my mother more after she died."

## Telling My Children

I sat my own children down and said, "I have something bad inside me, and the doctors are going to take it out to make me well." The mistake I made was not saying the words *breast cancer*. Brooks heard those words at school from a friend. He came home and said, "Mommy, my friend says you have breast cancer." My face turned red. I hadn't properly prepared my son. I thought I was shielding him by not saying the words *breast cancer*, so he had to hear it from someone else at school. We parents are here to teach and prepare our children for the rest of their lives. I didn't pass the test on that day. I should have been more up front with Brooks.

I tried to help them understand that the chemotherapy would cause me to lose my hair. I couldn't hide that from them, so I wanted to explain it. I said, "The medicine they give me to get rid of the cancer is so strong that it will cause me to lose my hair."

Both 7-year-old Brooks and 4-year-old Gabby said, "I don't want you to lose your hair." Conversations were often like echoes in my home.

Brooks the oldest usually said something first and Gabby would repeat it a second later.

I said, "Boys, I don't want to lose my hair either, but it will come back."

## Wigs, Baby

I even offered to let them help me pick out my wigs. One day I brought home three wigs to choose from. It turned into quite a wig party. All three boys put them on their heads and danced around like rock stars. I thought to myself, *so that's what my little girls would have looked like.* Three little blondes bounding around the room. We decided on one of the wigs for me and I said, "Okay, thanks for the help, guys." They were a part of a decision that had to do with my illness. Up until now, they probably felt helpless. At least this was something they could choose.

I tried to prepare them for the hair loss and cracked a bald joke every now and then to let them know it was going to be okay. But finally the day came when I realized I was losing my hair. In the back of my mind I had hoped to be the exception to the hair loss rule. But with adriamycin, you definitely lose your hair. I looked in the mirror and tried to do my "do" as I usually do…and voila, much of the do was in my brush. I looked around the bathroom and there were strands of hair all over the floor, in the bath tub, in the sink, on the counter. I had just swept it up that morning...but the hair continued to fall. It didn't come out in clumps, as I expected; it came out in strands.

I thought to myself, *I will be happy in September because my hair should be coming back in by then.* Then I had a revelation. Happy in September? Why wait to be happy? Why put off enjoying life, enjoying my children, just because I don't have hair? We aren't guaranteed tomorrow. We have to enjoy and appreciate today. Life is a gift and every single day is a gift.

This was early spring. I loved the spring and summer so much! I loved swimming with the kids and enjoying the summer. Why would I put off being happy until the fall? Right then and there I decided I would enjoy every single day no matter what. I would no longer have room in my life for getting upset over trivial problems. Life really was too short. I would accept the gift of each day with joy in my heart and gratitude.

## Lose Your Hair, Go for Pizza

Finally I decided to shave my head. That was something Dr. Cantrell suggested. He said many people choose to shave their heads when the hair starts to fall out. That way you're in control. Neither the cancer nor the chemo is in control of it. So I told my husband Doug it was time to shave my head. And to my surprise, he offered to shave it for me.

I thought I would cry and be upset. But the Lord allowed something absolutely wonderful to happen. We went to the For Ladies Only salon, where I had purchased a real hair wig. The owner understood cancer patients and had offered to buzz my head when the time was right. But on this day, the whole family arrived at her shop, and she welcomed us with open arms.

"I'll be glad to shave your head," she said with a smile.

"If it's okay," Doug said, "I'll do it."

I told the boys they could go out and watch cartoons if they wanted. While the younger two gravitated to the TV, my seven-year-old said, "No Mom, I want to stay in here." I wasn't sure if he was trying to support me or if it was just curiosity. Either way, I prayed that this would not traumatize him. Doug turned the clippers on and we both giggled.

I said, "Oh, now this could be dangerous."

I told him to leave about an inch all the way around. I thought I would cry and I thought this would be depressing. But it was actually wonderful. I had never felt more loving toward my husband.

We were closer than ever. In fact we got too close—my sweet husband nicked the back of my head. But we laughed about that, too. Doug also said he never felt closer to me. It was a loving moment.

Then I remember looking down at Brooks. I gasped when I realized he was gathering up my hair in his little hands and putting it in a plastic bag. I thought *Oh no, this was too much for my little boy.*

I said, "Honey, it'll be okay. Mommy's hair will come back, you don't have to save it."

He looked up at me with his big blue eyes and said, "No Mom, this is going to be great for show and tell!" Show and tell! Maybe he was a little too well adjusted! But I was grateful for his sweet, healthy outlook. It refreshed me to know he felt he could talk about this at school. He said, "Mom, will you come too?"

I asked, "Can I wear my wig?"

"Oh sure, Mom, you can wear your wig," he said with a smile.

## Show and Tell Mom

That night I was determined not to let the cancer rob me of a great Saturday night with my family. I popped on the wig after the buzz job, and we all went out for pizza. I didn't want to go home and cry. I wanted to show the children that this was no reason for despair. So we celebrated wig day.

Pizza has always marked major events in our lives, like birthdays. When Garrett was born, we had a pizza party in the hospital room, complete with Doug, my other two boys, and my parents.

By the way, I did end up going to show and tell that next week. The teacher pointed out I was the largest show and tell in the school's history. Once I was in front of the class, Brooks pointed out that I was wearing a wig...that I was really bald under all the fake hair. Some of the children raised their hands. I said, "Yes, what's your question?"

One little boy said, "My dad's bald, too!" Then child after child chimed in, "My dad is, too," or "My grandpa doesn't have any hair."

I felt like they had accepted me...being bald was okay.

Then we talked about being afraid, and I talked about the fact that I had been scared of going through the chemotherapy. I told them I realized after the treatments had started that the fear was worse than the treatment—it really wasn't so bad.

The children all agreed that their yearly check-ups, which for them includes a finger prick, weren't so bad after all. They realized that their fear was worse than actually going through it, because in an instant it was over.

# Life Goes On

Thanks be to God that life is going on! I thought life had returned to normal for my children. But almost a year after the diagnosis, I was sitting at the breakfast table discussing whether I would work on the elementary school yearbook. Brooks, then eight, piped in, "Mommy, I don't think you should do that because you had cancer and you are weak."

I had to work to keep my jaw from dropping open. This child was more affected by the cancer than I had realized. Just a month before, I had some reconstruction revisions. That surgery did cause me to avoid lifting and I had to hold off on running for a month. But I was better now. I was training for a marathon! But my little boy still saw Mommy as weak and ravaged by cancer. I said, "Honey, Mommy is better now. I'm strong. I can run and jump and even do the school yearbook."

I pray for all the children of cancer victims. We will never know just how deep the scars go. It's hard to watch Mommy lose her hair, watch Mommy go to bed in the middle of the day, watch Mommy take medicine to keep her from getting sick. I pray God will make them stronger as a result of this, more compassionate, more caring about others.

I remember the gentleness my seven-year-old

showed me when I was recovering from surgery. He softly touched my arm and carefully kissed me so as not to hurt me. This was the same kid who tackled me at the front door each night I arrived home for dinner! Brooks and Gabby both helped deliver goodies into the bedroom. They especially liked baskets. One basket in particular had children's books in it. What a perfect gift. The children snuggled gently in my bed and I read the books. I couldn't do much Mommy duty, but I could lay there and read!

I hope I'm a better mother as a result of the cancer. I now try not to put off doing the things that really matter. My list of things to do this summer includes: going to the beach, building sandcastles, planting flowers, planting vegetables, going horseback riding, setting up a lemonade stand, and just laughing and enjoying my family.

## Interviews with My Children

While I was driving Brooks and Gabby to friends' houses a year after my surgery, I showed Brooks some pages I was working on for this book. He read the first page. Since he loves to read, he is a great reader. He said, "It's good." That meant so much!

"Brooks," I said, "Could I interview you for the

book? I think it could help other kids who have Moms with cancer." Brooks said, "Sure!" So here's part of our interview.

**Mom:** Brooks, how did you feel when I came home and told you I had something bad inside my body?

**Brooks:** It was scary.

**Mom:** What did you think was going to happen?

**Brooks:** I thought you were going to die (he said solemnly).

**Mom:** But we never said I was going to die; why did you think that?

**Brooks:** I don't know, I guess because you were in the hospital. I thought you were really, really sick.

**Mom:** How did I act?

**Brooks:** You were crying a lot and I figured something was wrong with you.

**Mom:** I thought I hid my crying from you; I guess I didn't.

**Brooks:** No, because I heard you crying in your room sometimes.

**Mom:** What if I didn't tell you I was sick and you heard me crying, what would you think then?

**Brooks:** Probably think like your dad, Pap-Pap, died or something.

**Mom:** Would it have been more scary if I didn't tell you what was happening?

**Brooks:** Yes.

**Mom:** Why?

**Brooks:** Because I wouldn't feel good if you didn't tell me what was happening.

**Mom:** Do you remember Mommy sitting on the floor in your room and talking to you and Gabby?

**Brooks:** Yes.

**Mom:** What do you remember about that conversation?

**Brooks:** You said there was something bad inside of you. I asked if you were going to die.

**Mom:** Do you remember when I said the doctors were going to take out the bad thing so that I would be okay?

**Brooks:** Yes. I remember you saying God would wrap His arms around us and help you be safe. He'd help me not worry and all that.

**Mom:** Did He?

**Brooks:** Yes.

**Mom:** How?

**Brooks:** He helped me not worry, then you survived. I felt real confident after that.

**Mom:** How do you feel now that cancer's behind us?

**Brooks:** I feel fine. I know you'll never get it again.

**Mom:** I don't think I'll ever get it again, either. But isn't it nice knowing that in any bad thing God can help us through?

**Brooks:** Yes.

**Mom:** How did you feel when I told you I was going to lose my hair?

**Brooks:** I was really freaked out, I didn't know what you'd look like without your hair.

**Mom:** Is there anything that I said that helped you with that?

**Brooks:** Yes, you said your hair would grow back.

**Mom:** Did me wearing wigs bother you?

**Brooks:** Your hair (wig) didn't look the same really; it looked real puffy.

**Mom:** Did you like it when my hair was coming back?

**Brooks:** Yes, I felt really good. I thought you were getting better as your hair grew back.

**Mom:** A year later you thought I was still weak. Why?

**Brooks:** Because you had to go to chemotherapy and all that stuff.

**Mom:** So now that I ran the marathon and did your school year book, do you still think I'm weak?

**Brooks:** NO!

Here's part of my interview with 5-year-old Gabby.

**Mom:** How did you feel when I said I had something bad inside me?

**Gabby:** I thought you wouldn't be around to read
stories.

**Mom:** Were you scared?

**Gabby:** No.

**Mom:** Was it because we prayed and I said God
would take care of us?

**Gabby:** Yes.

**Mom:** Did Mommy look funny when you came to
see me at the hospital?

**Gabby:** Not really, but what was that breath tube
for?

**Mom:** It helped me get better. It gave me air to
breathe.

**Gabby:** I liked the flowers.

**Mom:** Did it upset you when I lost my hair?

**Gabby:** No, I liked seeing all those funny wigs. I
like the orange one. The curly one. It was funny
when it was hanging up there at the place.

**Mom:** What was it like seeing Mommy without
hair?

**Gabby:** I wanted you to put your wig on.

**Mom:** When did you know Mommy was all better?
**Gabby:** When you had hair, like you do now.

I look back fondly on the time when I could only lay there and read a book to my children, or sit in a chair and watch them play. That was a special time for all of us.

# Chapter Nine

# *God's Comfort Through So Many*

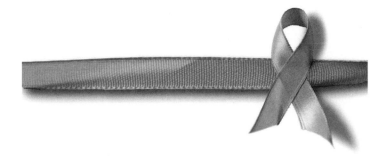

*T*wo days after my diagnosis, Doug and I came home to see my friend Lisa's car in the drive-way. I thought, *God sends people when you need them.* I was blown away by the news I had cancer. But being greeted by two longtime friends, Lisa and our children's nanny Nessa, brought a bit of comfort.

Lisa sat down and told me how she felt when her son was diagnosed with a brain tumor. She told me about her faith and how much stronger it got. We sat for a long time. I was stunned but felt like she was an angel sitting next to me. Nessa sat across from me and said, "It will be okay." Somehow when she said that, just like my children, I believed her. These two women were both strong in their faith, and I knew their prayers were already going up for me.

Lisa handed me a Catholic medal. She knew I wasn't Catholic, but she said, "Take this. During Joey's brain tumor I felt like this protected us." Today I was gaining strength from Lisa. She had walked through the fire more than a year before this. She had made it and said her faith brought her through. She said she was stronger. I realized that the Holy Spirit worked through Lisa that day to make it bearable.

That day was the first of many comforting moments, thanks to others. When I decided to make my cancer battle public, I never imagined that the response would be so great. I simply wanted to warn people, but instead many viewers reached out to me. It was as if God was reaching out to me through so many.

Proverbs 11:25 teaches us that "*he who refreshes others will himself be refreshed.*" It was true. I received thousands of cards and letters. I was overwhelmed that so many people would spend the money and time to let me know that a total stranger cared. These Bible verses were just what I needed to hear at the time. Isaiah 43:2 assured me, "*When you pass through the waters, I will be with you; and when you pass through the rivers, they will not sweep over you. When you walk through the fire, you will not be burned.*"

God continued to speak to me through so many people in the community. Cards, letters, and gifts poured in through the mail. I had to pass on the hope I clung to in those encouraging words from friends, family, and total strangers. But now the strangers even felt like family members.

Women wrote letters that started, "I know you're not my daughter, although I feel as if you are." How powerful to have a bond with people I've never even met! God is so good.

In other letters there were Scriptures and stories of survival. Many wrote that they had been there before me. They too had cancer and survived. Some were five-year survivors, some were ten-year survivors, and others were fifteen- and twenty-year survivors. That was so encouraging, because I thought that if others could survive before me, then I could do it, too!

Other letters read: "Dear Brenda, I'm praying

for your complete recovery."

"Brenda, our prayers are with you at this time. We miss you."

"Brenda, may the Lord comfort you, care for you, and restore good health to you soon. We look forward to seeing your sweet smile real soon!"

"Dear Brenda, please know that every thought of you carries along with it a prayer for your health and well-being."

"Mrs. Ladun, I am so sorry to hear that you have breast cancer. I am thinking about you and praying for you. I watch you on the news and you are like part of my family."

"You are remembered in prayer. God is a wonderful, intimate friend, and He hears the prayers of your heart."

In Isaiah 46:4, God says, *"I will carry you; I will sustain you and I will rescue you."* God certainly was carrying me through. He was reaching out to me through so many people. I especially liked the letters that talked about surviving against the odds. One man wrote that he thought he'd lost his wife after she had a heart attack. But a miracle brought her back to life. He prayed hard for that miracle, and it was granted. There is power in prayer, and I felt that prayer working in my life.

Thanks for the encouragement! It meant more

than you could possibly know. It put a smile on my face.

## Covered-Dish Heaven

Those first few weeks after surgery, not only did the cards and letters with Bible verses and words of encouragement lift me up, but meals were delivered to our front door. My sister Linda loved to find out what had magically shown up for dinner. That was God's love pouring through a community.

Then there were the baskets filled with goodies. The boys loved these the most! One day they were in awe of a basket that came from a local radio duo, Russ and Dee Fine. It was a basket made to look like a hot air balloon, filled with chocolates. The largest basket came from my friends at my Jazzercise class. It barely fit through the front door. It contained everything from socks to chocolates. Each card, gift, and flower arrangement or plant was so special. So many people let me know they cared. I've always wondered, *How could God love so many people?* Now I understand, because I witnessed His love pouring through so many. That love lifted me up. It was an important part of my spiritual healing.

Fourteen weeks after the surgery, life started to get back to normal and it was time to run errands.

(I want to warn you about driving for the first time after a mastectomy. The pain can grab you that first time you fire up those pectoral muscles after the operation, when you turn the steering wheel.) Within two days of running errands, I was overwhelmed with stories from people on the street. I'd shared, now others were sharing with me in ways I'd never imagined.

## *Shared Courage Helped Me Go On*

Often when we think we can't go on, God says, *Yes, you can.* Matthew 19:26 says, *"with God all things are possible."* We learn from 2 Corinthians 12:9 that, *"My grace is sufficient for you, for My power is made perfect in weakness."* And Philippians 4:13 helps us to know, *"I can do everything through Him who gives me strength."*

Faith and friends do provide strength during the tough times. Other cancer survivors provide solace like no one else can. When I talk with some of my new friends who are cancer survivors, I feel like we've been friends all our lives. Imagine the person you run to in a crisis. That's how I feel about my new friends that have also survived cancer.

This letter meant so much to me. She said everything I needed to hear at the time.

*April 4, 2001*

*Hi Brenda:*

*I wanted to share with you my experience when I started losing my hair in the hopes that it may help you as well. It was about 12 days after I had my first chemo treatment of adriamycin and cytoxan. My husband noticed one Sunday morning that there was more hair than usual on my robe. I ran my fingers through my hair and I had several loose strands in my hand. The next day I sat in front of my mirror and stared at my head, because I knew I would look like this for nearly a year. I had to look beyond that shaved head and look toward healing. I immediately put on my wig and went about my business. We females take such pride in our hair and it's a disturbing feeling, but this too will pass.*

*I share your feelings right now. All of us who have been through chemotherapy know each step you are taking. You are not alone. Please don't hesitate to reach out to any of us if you need a buddy to talk to. God bless you; I continue to keep you in my prayers.*

*Regards,*
*Paula McCoy*

That letter gives me such a sense of peace every time I read it. Even now, a year after my surgery, it helps. There's nothing like listening to someone who's been there and survived to provide strength. And there were so many other cards and letters that offered hope and good advice about being your own health advocate. For example, read this letter from Jean Motte; she asked me to share it with others to hopefully help someone else.

---

*April 9, 2001*

*Dear Brenda,*

*Brenda, because of the opportunity you have of communicating to so many people, I am telling you my story so that you might use it. My lump was found on an annual gynecological visit. I was advised to return in two months, which I did. The doctor did a needle aspiration without success. I also had a mammogram, which was read as "normal." My doctor advised me to return in six months. During these six months, I was experiencing some aching under my arm, but I was too busy to think about it. By January 1996, I was beginning to have an uneasy feeling about this lump, but again I put my*

---

*feelings on the back burner because of a family cri-sis. By the time I went back for the six month check-up, my doctor said, "You need to see a surgeon." I knew that this lump was a malignant one.*

*Brenda, I do not place all of the blame for this "watch and wait" approach on my doctor. I am a nurse and my husband is a retired physician. I should have gone with my gut feeling and the knowledge I had and insisted on earlier removal of the lump. The message I would like for you to get out to the public is to pay attention to their bodies and their own feelings. Get a lump or any other unusu-al growth out of their body as soon as possible.*

*The neatest thing about this experience is that I developed a more intimate relationship with God. Oh, I had been busy doing His work at church, going on medical missions trips, and so on. But after coming face to face with my own mortality, rela-tionships with family, friends, and people in gener-al became more important to me than ever before. All of God's creation became so precious to me. I hope and pray I never lose the perspective I gained from this experience.*
*In Christian love,*
*Jean Motte*

What Jean said was perfect! Her warning to others about being diligent about an unusual spot or growth on the body is so important. I've had many other cancer survivors tell me similar stories. Their cancer was not detected at first, but they had a nagging feeling that something was wrong. That nagging feeling is something I felt about the changes in my breasts.

Being able to talk about breast cancer with others who've been there is so important. Sharing with fellow breast cancer survivors gave me so much courage. Hearing about people five, ten, and even thirty years after their cancer battle infused me with hope and a stronger will that I, too, could beat it.

After giving a speech to a group of cancer survivors at The Church of Brook Highlands, I received this e-mail from one of the members of that support group.

*Hello Brenda,*

*My daughter, Crystal, has walked with her parents through three battles with cancer—I have had breast cancer and endometrial cancer, and my husband has a brain tumor. She has turned her struggle of dealing with her parent's cancer into something positive. Last year she started a support group at her middle school for children who have a loved one with cancer. Well, she wanted to do more. She contacted the American Cancer Society and the Alabama Foundation of Oncology, and this summer, with their support, will hold a day camp for these children. The camp will be free to children. It will be held on June 23 at YMCA Camp Hargis.*

*Brenda, thank you again for your testimony. It made me want to go out and let others know that you can fight it. Just turn it over to God. He will be beside you. We will be praying for you.*

*Carmen Bedwell*

Thank you to every person who wrote a letter of encouragement! Those letters helped me know I could go on. We can make it. We can be better than before. We can have a close walk with God. We can also live life to its fullest, because we have faced death.

## Find a Mentor

If you don't have a mentor—someone you can pick up the phone and talk to about cancer fears—find one. Talking about it is so important. If you don't know of someone, you can contact the American Cancer Society; they have programs and chat rooms that can help get you in touch with others.

I was lucky enough to build my own support group from people I knew in my neighborhood, at my child's school, and at the hospital. You'd think after the last treatment, I might not need to keep getting help from others. But the truth is you can never really let go of that support system. Nine months after my first surgery I had to reach out to another one of those positive survivors. After my last procedure for reconstruction, I felt like I was on a mountaintop all alone. This was it. I'd made it, but now what? No more procedures to schedule, no next phase to look forward to.

It was a strange feeling. I thought I'd be jumping up and down, because it was over. But I guess I was like a person who's been trapped in a dark cave for a long time. I came out, and the sun was too bright. I had to adjust. The last procedure is a tattoo to give color to the reconstructed nipples. The day after that, I felt the need to talk to Karen Jackson. She had been my mentor throughout the cancer experience. Her surgery and chemotherapy preceded mine by a matter of weeks.

"Hello Karen, it's Brenda. How are you?" I asked. Believe me, when one cancer survivor asks another how they are, it's not small talk. I usually hold my breath and pray they will say they're okay...and she did. This teacher offered me strength and hope all along the way. When I was terrified of the chemotherapy, she said, "Hey, it's not so bad, just a lot like morning sickness when you're pregnant." That made it seem do-able. When I was in my hospital bed after surgery, Karen showed me, even though my arm was sore, that soon I'd be able to lift my arm just like she could. And when my hair was about to fall out from the chemotherapy, she gave me tips for buying a wig and counseled me on how it would feel emotionally.

Karen was a perfect stranger before I had cancer. Now I feel like she's a sister. Now that I'd made it to the top of the mountain, I needed to talk to

Karen about this feeling. I was stunned that it was all over. During the surgeries, I felt protected. I was closely watched and could consult with my doctors. Now I was like a little bird being pushed out of the nest. The security of that doctor's office would be gone. "So Karen," I asked, "did it feel strange after you were finished with the reconstruction?" She agreed it did, and said also the tattoos were a little bright at first but would fade with time.

Karen Jackson was one of many mentors God sent my way. I believe God sent each one to deliver a different message. I developed relationships with other survivors: my new friend the teacher who continued to walk every day and travel with her husband during chemo, the other teacher at my son's school who didn't miss work because she didn't want to let the kids down, the tri-athlete who kept competing through chemo, the woman who counseled me on strategies to overcome digestive woes.

All these stories of strong and positive cancer survivors helped. I thought if they can do it, then so can I.

*Chapter Ten*

# Every Day Is a Gift

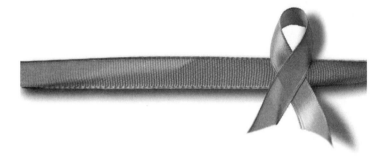

$\mathcal{N}$ow, just three days before what I hope will be my last chemo treatment, I feel like a long distance swimmer who has almost made it to shore after being tossed about by a rough sea. It feels as if I can now stand against the crashing waves as I step closer and closer to shore. Every day I wonder if the stormy sea will really calm down, and I wonder what life will be like in six months.

*Just one more time, God willing, I'll have to*

*endure the pokes and prods of the nurse searching*
*for a vein that hasn't yet collapsed from a previous*
*treatment. Hopefully I only have one more time to*
*feel the cold chill as the solution enters my veins,*
*along with the burn and sting of the drugs.*

*I hope and pray I will never lose the wonderful*
*perspective on life God has revealed to me through*
*breast cancer. I want to continue to seize every*
*moment and praise God for every day and appreci-*
*ate all the beautiful things life offers. What's more*
*precious than the sound of my children laughing, or*
*contentedly sitting next to the man I love and just*
*enjoying the sound of him breathing?*

I thank God for every day. Every day is a great day. I often hum the song my son learned last year in a chapel service, "This is the day that the Lord has made, let us rejoice and be glad in it."

I hope and pray the cancer does not show up somewhere else in my body because, as Dr. Cantrell says, once it metastasizes there is no cure. "It's treatable?" I asked, trying to look for hope.

"Oh yes," he said, "it's treatable."

And that's where many find hope. Some researchers believe the key to dealing with cancer is not always looking for a cure but treating it like many other diseases are treated. Controlling the cancer and preventing it from growing any further, some believe, is the most important approach for successfully battling cancer.

*"He said to his disciples, 'Why are you so afraid? Do you still have no faith?'"*
—Mark 4:40

Is my future uncertain? Here on earth it certainly is. We have today but are not guaranteed tomorrow. I'm constantly reminded there is always a chance the cancer could come back. If I call my dentist about a toothache, he tells me it's probably just an infected wisdom tooth. But we have to watch it since I've had cancer. Or if I call a doctor about my back hurting because I ran too much, the doctor says, "We'll take a look at it after you've had a bone scan." Headaches will never be the same again. I pause not because of the pain, but because of the thought that this could be cancer. I knew I could go crazy wondering if the cancer had spread to the brain. It's all too much for one human being to handle mentally. But the great thing is, we don't have to handle it. We can give those worries to God. Let Him handle it!

*"Then Jesus said to his disciples: 'Therefore I tell you, do not worry about your life, what*

*you will eat; or about your body, what you will wear. Life is more than food, and the body more than clothes....Who of you by worrying can add a single hour to his life?'"*
—Luke12: 22–25

God has a plan for all our lives; we just need to trust Him and go along for the ride. As I have learned to say, you may be pleasantly surprised to find some of your worst problems also reveal your greatest blessings.

## *Endings Good and Bad*

The last treatment came and went. What a relief to be able to walk out of the cancer center and be free of treatments, hopefully forever! As the months passed, some of the shock of having cancer faded. But six months later, even though I was more secure with my health after my doctor told me I was in fact in remission, I still felt like I was walking on eggshells.

I have to pinch myself every now and then and say, Yes, it's real. I don't have to go to chemo today? What a great day. Six months after the end of chemo, I'm grateful for all I learned through the cancer experience.

*"Praise the Lord, O my soul, and forget not*

*all his benefits—who forgives all your sins and heals all your diseases, who redeems your life from the pit and crowns you with love and compassion." —Psalm 103:2–4*

Speaking of love and compassion, because I've been faced with a deadly disease and the possibility it could return, I have learned a deeper love and compassion for those who are suffering and have suffered from disease. I want to wipe away their pain. I want to give a reassuring hug that everything will be better. That's what an uncertain future has done for me.

Why do some people survive cancer and others do not? I don't know. But I do know we can't possibly fathom what God's plan includes. However, we are assured that He loves us and has prepared a better place for those who love Him.

Survivors' long-term stories are so encouraging. But at the same time, I have to brace myself for some of the not-so-encouraging stories. I'd like to forget the fact that cancer is a killer.

I think, in the beginning, my friends and family wouldn't tell me any bad cancer news. A beautiful middle-aged woman was a member of my country club. She had a glow about her and emitted class and a sense of peace every time I saw her. She had battled breast cancer and beat it. Then she battled kidney cancer. I ran into her at a luncheon one day. It was during my chemo, and I was wearing my wig. With a big warm smile, she said, "We need to sit down and talk sometime."

I said, "I'd really like that."

Again the voice of my mother rings in my head. She always used to say, "Never put off until tomorrow what you can do today."

That lunch never took place. Shortly after our conversation, she became very ill from her battle with kidney cancer. Months later she passed away. No one told me, even though they knew I had talked with her. I guess some of my friends thought they were protecting me. But the reality is, now that I've been through a battle for my life, I want to support the family members of cancer victims. I feel a connection with them.

It was a blow to hear about this woman losing her battle, but it was a fact. I prayed for her family. I knew she was spiritually prepared, because I talked with her in the parking lot after church one Sunday. She said, "I don't know how anyone gets through a major illness without faith." I agreed that it was the only thing that got me through the cancer battle. We parted, and I prayed for God to heal her. But the earthly healing never came. God has a plan. It was time to call her home.

It hurts when another cancer patient loses that battle. It's like we have a connection. It's like losing a member of the team.

We don't know why some people live on and beat cancer while others fall to its devastating blow. But without the reality that cancer could claim my life, I wouldn't have started really living. I mean living life to its fullest, enjoying every day and savoring time with family and friends.

I look at my children and hug them and tell them, "Mommy's love will always live inside your heart." I want to make a difference in the lives of those I speak to at churches and meeting halls.

As far as my uncertain future is concerned...I know my *spiritual* future is secure. I asked Jesus into my heart when I was 12 years old. I later renewed my vow as an adult. Jesus Christ is my Lord and Savior. I trust Him with all my heart and commit my life to Him. Cancer as an adult brought me to my knees and made me realize just how wonderful God's grace is to save a sinner and promise everlasting life.

I'm certain that I'll go to heaven one day. That's the most important part of the big picture. Even though we have to deal with the uncertainty that the cancer might return, I have confidence that when it's my time, I'll go to a better place.

> *"Therefore we do not lose heart. Though outwardly we are wasting away, yet inwardly we are being renewed day by day. For our light and momentary troubles are achieving for us an eternal glory that far outweighs them all. So we fix our eyes not on what is seen, but on what is unseen. For what is seen is temporary, but what is unseen is eternal."*
> —2 Corinthians 4:16–18

## The Best Thing

Life goes on, not only for myself but for my family as well. Since my recovery from my battle with cancer, I've felt like a kid in a candy store. My husband probably thinks I'm a little nuts, but he indulges me.

I often ask during my speeches, "Are there any psychologists, psychiatrists, or counselors in the room?" Usually someone raises a hand. "After this next statement, you'll want to set up an appointment for me, but…

"Cancer is the best thing that ever happened to me!"

If you're a survivor, you probably know what I'm talking about. I want to squeeze every ounce out of the day that I can. I want to get up in the morning and run, play tennis, go to the park or zoo with the kids, and have lunch with my hubby or a dear friend, then go on to ABC 33/40 and deliver the news to the best of my ability.

I also make a point now to cook for someone who is sick. Those meals while I was down kept me and my family going and meant so much to us. Even on the busiest of days, I try harder now to rearrange my schedule to attend a funeral.

While attending a funeral for the father of a friend of mine, I found some comfort in the fact that life goes on. This strong marine had battled cancer valiantly for many years. Finally the cancer won. I thought, *it really is in God's hands*. He's the One who allows us each day. While sitting in the pew at the funeral home, I watched people fill the seats one by one. Most people were solemn, some were sniffling and crying. But one group of young ladies in their late teens or early 20s helped me realize life does go on. They were trying hard to be respectful. But before the service, they started chatting as if they were at a luncheon. Life does go on.

Then while we were at the grave, I noticed something else. At this cemetery in Trussville, Alabama, we stood high up on a hill. The view was beautiful. But while life had ended here on earth for the father of my friend, I could see the traffic and the hustle and bustle below on Highway 11. Life goes on; it has to. Even though it's painful to say goodbye to a loved one, life is too precious to waste. And somehow that lifted my spirits; I know that I have battled a killer, and when God decides my time has come, my family and friends will go on. They have to; that's life. How good to know that even if we can't be here on this earth, they will go on to enjoy and live life! We each have a life to live and we must live it. I hope to pass on the joy of life to my children. God wants us all to experience that joy.

Jesus says in Matthew 13:44, *"The kingdom of heaven is like treasure hidden in a field. When a man found it, he hid it again, and then in his joy went and sold all he had and bought that field."*

God wants us to discover that joy.

## Things to Do...

That's why I want to embrace all the things I told myself before cancer I was gonna do, but never got around to doing. Now I just do them.

One morning after running for 45 minutes, I was hot and sweaty. I looked at the pool and jumped in, clothes and all. The kids got a big laugh out of that. Especially because I took off my hat with hair and revealed my bald head. You ain't seen nothing till you've seen a bald lady swim, I often joked.

But it's that perspective on life I wouldn't trade for anything in the world.

I want to fill my days with those precious moments like listening to our two older sons tell jokes that don't make any sense.

I want to watch my baby, who's 22 months, giggle and run as he tries to snatch my wig.

I want to look at my husband and chuckle when the kids are being kids.

That's how I choose to spend my days. I want to be there and take the call from the woman who's just been diagnosed with cancer. I want to raise money to defeat a killer. That's how I fill my days. I want to fill them with what's important in life.

I want to make a difference...to be there for friends and loved ones.

## And Not to Do...

What I now choose not to do is to stress over the little things that in the end don't matter. If I'm stuck in traffic, I say, "So what? I'll get there when I get there, and all the stressing in the world won't get me there sooner." I want to push out the little disagreements that can sour a precious moment.

I now get rid of shoes that hurt my feet. (Why

didn't I do that before?) I'd let them clutter my closet and cringe every time I put them on, all in the name of fashion? No thanks, life is too short to be uncomfortable for no reason. I choose not to stress over my hair or devote half a day making sure it's just right. My life is much more than hair. Bad hair days don't dictate whether or not I'm going to have a bad day.

Do you have a top ten stress list? I did, and since my cancer battle, it's changed dramatically. For example, 1 being the least stressful and 10 being the most stressful, a 10 on the stress list used to be traffic jams and broken appliances. But since facing off with death toe to toe, my list looks like this: 10 is now a death in the family, 9 is a life and death situation, 8 is a serious illness, 7 is a minor illness, 6 is a job loss or family crisis (this would have been 10 before my cancer diagnosis), 5 is a financial crisis, 4 is a broken appliance or home repair ( this would have been a 10 before as well), 3 would be a traffic jam, 2 would be a forgotten child's note to the teacher, and 1 is a bad hair day.

Before cancer, I wouldn't set life's frustrations aside and choose not to stress about them, as I do now. Now, I can't be bothered about small things. Enjoy life! God wants that joy in your life.

*"Shout for joy to the Lord, all the earth.*

*Worship the Lord with gladness; come before him with joyful songs. Know that the Lord is God. It is he who made us, and we are his; we are his people, the sheep of his pasture."*
—Psalm 100:1–3

I ask you to do something for you and me today. Look outside and appreciate the world God made for us. Listen to the birds in the morning. Take time with your loved ones, and don't stress over things that really don't matter in the big picture. Be kind to others. Pray for your own health and the health of others. Pray unceasingly. Let the Lord guide you and lead you. Find your own gift in life and share it with others. When you start focusing on other people and their needs, you get so much more in return.

Don't waste a minute or put off those important tasks, like cooking for a friend in need. Take an active role in protecting your own health. Do monthly self breast exams, get yearly clinical exams, and get that mammogram. Remember your own health; don't get too busy for yourself while you're taking care of the rest of the world.

Remember, our families and friends are much more important than tasks. Our help to others is what really makes the world go round. And that's what lasts beyond our own lives.

## Disney World

One year and one month after the surgery, we planned the trip to Disney World that we had to cancel the year before. This trip represented a victory, much like the victory of crossing the finish line in the marathon. What cancer had robbed from my family the year before we would reclaim this year. We would be able to heal and bond as a family. I would take the advice of the mother I'd talked to at a school hot dog supper. She said that after beating tongue cancer, she and her family took some time off to *be* a family again.

So look out Disney, here we come! Watch out Mickey, the Bell boys are in the Magic Kingdom! And for the time being, Mommy has reclaimed her throne as Mommy. But life hadn't really returned to normal, I realized. Life was better than before, better than normal. When you realize how short life really is, you can embrace it. Life is a gift.

## Thoughts to Keep

The Sunday before we left for our Florida vacation, Buddy Gray, our pastor at Hunter Street Baptist Church, preached about living life as if you knew you were going to die soon. I could imagine it very easily. A year ago, I thought I might die soon. That's when life changed and became much sweeter to me.

Here are some notes I took during Buddy's sermon that I hope will help you have a richer life. I know the Holy Spirit was speaking to me. It's an important message for us all.

• Psalm 90:12 (TLB)— *"Teach us to number our days and recognize how few they are; help us to spend them as we should."* Choose what you do carefully. Time is precious.

• Ephesians 5:15 (TEV)— *"So be careful how you live. Don't live like ignorant people, but like wise people."* Figure out what is a waste of time in your life and throw it out. Worry, frustration, regret, and procrastination can eat up your days. Is that really how you want to spend your precious time?

• Ephesians 5:17 (TEV)— *"Don't be fools, then, but try to find out what the Lord wants you to do."* Focus on God's plan for your life. If I'd focused on myself and what I lost because of breast cancer, I'd probably still be depressed. But thank God I could focus on something much more important: His plan for my life.

• Ephesians 5:19–20 (TEV)— *"Speak to one anoth-*

er with the words of psalms, hymns, and sacred songs; sing hymns and psalms to the Lord with praise in your hearts. In the name of our Lord Jesus Christ, always give thanks for everything to God the Father." Be filled with God's presence. And maintain a positive attitude. Bad attitudes are the worst time-wasters. Appreciate each day you have.

• Galatians 5:22–23 (NIV)— "But the fruit of the Spirit is love, joy, peace, patience, kindness, goodness, faithfulness, gentleness and self-control. Against such things there is no law." Let the Spirit bear fruit in your life—it's possible in every situation.

My prayer is that this book provided you with some peace during a turbulent time. Remember we will always be faced with problems, big and small. But you can hold onto the fact that you are not alone, that others have gone through the same thing, and that others care for you. And most of all, God's Holy Spirit will help you through every fearful situation, every challenge, every moment. Whatever happens, you can trust in Him.

# Defining Moments— Doug Bell's Story

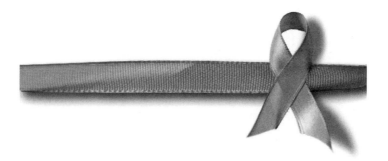

There are defining moments in everyone's life. Some are seemingly small events that happen as part of everyday life and some are clearly very big events. As a sportscaster, I report all the time on athletes who experience life-changing events in their fields. There are defining moments...and then there is learning that your wife has breast cancer.

The day Brenda's breast cancer was diagnosed was a defining moment for me. The woman I call my BW (Beautiful Wife) called me on my cell phone and asked me to meet her at her doctor's office. Not until that call, when I detected something in her voice, did I understand the complexity and seriousness of what we were about to go through together.

Since that day, I have become much more emotional about things. I warn people, when I'm out making a speech to a civic organization or church group, that I tend to get emotional when I talk about my wife. I used to make fun of Dick Vermeil, the coach of the Kansas City Chiefs, who would tear up and cry about his team's ups and downs. I can no longer make fun of him. My wife has changed me.

I believe more than ever that life is good. For all the negative things in our world, I'm a witness that there is so much good in the hearts of our fellow men. People who know me are probably shaking their heads right now to hear me going on like this and being so sentimental. Is this the same guy who watches Sportscenter on a daily basis, memorizes the USA Today sports page, and agonizes over a missed birdie putt on the eighteenth hole? Yes, it's the same me, but my life has changed, and the way I see things has changed. Some people call it growing up. I'm not sure how to describe it.

# A Husband's Decision

One defining moment came during Brenda's surgery. I had to make a decision for Brenda while she was under anesthesia. Her surgeon, Dr. Winchester, came out after the right breast was removed and explained that the cancer was more widespread than they had thought. We had discussed this possibility beforehand, and now they were asking me for permission to perform a double mastectomy. I looked at Dr. Snowden and asked simply, "What do you think?" She responded that if she were choosing for herself, she would want it done. There was a strong likelihood that the cancer would show up in the left breast if it were not removed. I already knew the answer, but it's good to get confirmation from someone you trust. I agreed and signed the consent forms to perform the procedure. To be there for Brenda, to make this very personal decision on her behalf, to do everything I could for her well being, was a powerful thing for me. Defining moments, indeed.

Dr. Winchester returned once more to explain that the second surgery went well and that she also removed some cancerous lymph nodes. She felt that it was best if I didn't mention the double mastectomy right away to Brenda. She would tell Brenda after she came out of the fog of anesthesia. I agreed, but reserved the right to change my mind.

As the reconstructive part of the surgery was being completed, I flipped on the television to ABC 33/40 news to watch the message Brenda had taped to be run during her surgery. I can't describe the feeling that was running through my body. There was the love of my life, telling of her diagnosis and urging other people to get checked. Tears were streaming down my face. I couldn't hold it in any longer. What an incredibly strong woman. How angelic she appeared as she looked into the camera with those gorgeous green eyes, urging people to fight this dreaded disease.

I had no idea what an impact Brenda's taped message would have. Her decision was absolutely the right one. To this day, I am stopped by total strangers who tell me that their lives have been changed because of what my wife did. What a blessing! I'll never forget that night, the announcement, the tears of joy.

## Brenda's Toughness

I remember when I played football in a 9th-grade championship game, when our best defensive lineman broke his hand early in the game. Our coach, who had been a medic in Vietnam, took pride in being able to tape up his troops and get them back on the field. He grabbed the young man's hand, placed a tennis ball in his palm, and proceeded to wrap several rolls of tape around the hand. The kid cried through the whole procedure, but he played the rest of the game. I was only 13 years old, but that made a lasting impression on me.

That kid was the toughest son of a gun I had ever seen until I witnessed my wife fighting her way through chemotherapy. I remember when Dr. Cantrell, the oncologist, explained to Brenda that most people don't go to work after a chemotherapy treatment. Most people just rest after the 90-minute treatment. With that determined look in her eye, Brenda told both of us that she was not going to let this take away her normal life. That meant she wasn't going to miss any work, any field trips for the kids, or anything else because of her chemo treatments. Dr. Cantrell said something like, "Why don't we wait and see," but he had never met anyone with the ironclad single-handed determination of my wife.

I went with Brenda to all of her chemo visits, and I marveled at how she approached this agonizing procedure every time. When we showed up in the lobby, she was recognized by almost everyone. As we waited, she would sit and talk with someone about their cancer story, comforting them and reassuring them it would be okay. I often wondered, as I sat and watched her relate to these cancer patients, if Brenda was somehow placed in this situation for a reason. She has a unique way of making total strangers feel like long-lost friends. Every time we entered the lobby, she knew she would be facing that painful attack on her left arm, and then the chemo drug that would wear down her body; yet she found so much joy and exhilaration in helping others. She helped me see what's really important. Those were defining moments.

## Shaving Brenda's Hair

Brenda tried to keep from losing her hair, but one Saturday she brought me her favorite hat and showed me the handfuls of blonde hair inside it. She had lost this battle, and we decided that it was time to go ahead and shave it off. I asked her if I could do the honors. Brooks had a baseball game that day, so we decided to do it afterwards and then go out to dinner as a family, as we usually did after a ballgame.

As I picked up the electric clippers at our friend's hair salon, I must admit I became a little nervous. I realized I was about to shave the head of my gorgeous wife. Talk about a surreal moment. As her beautiful blonde locks quietly fell to the floor, I couldn't believe what I was doing or what I was witnessing. I felt a twinge of guilt, but that was silly. It would be either me or someone else with the clippers. Brenda smiled and gazed into the mirror. She rubbed her cleanly-shaven head and said she liked the way it felt. I gave her a kiss and a hug and told her how much I loved her. It was a new level of closeness for us.

## Believing in Prayer

Last summer, while I was covering the Southeastern Conference baseball tournament in Birmingham, a gentleman stopped me and inquired how Brenda was feeling. He and his family, who had been through a similar experience with his daughter, had been praying for us. I had never met this man, yet we talked like we were old friends. He explained how Brenda's fight against cancer had really helped his daughter battle through her physical and mental anguish. This wasn't the last time this has happened to me. I've learned that people are so kind and that prayer is a powerful thing.

My father suffered his second heart attack the week of Brenda's third reconstructive surgery. That week I commuted from Birmingham to Atlanta, and spent a lot of time meditating and talking to God in the hospital chapels. Thanks to the good Lord and talented surgeons, both procedures went well. I really believe in my heart that God answered my prayers.

I find myself seeking and appreciating quiet time these days. I collect my thoughts, give thanks to God, and pray for the health and well being of my family and friends. This is good for the soul, and believe me, it works.

Right now, there is no reason to think Brenda will ever have cancer again. We are approaching it one day, one month, one year at a time. There are no guarantees, but we are living life to the fullest. Each day is so exciting.

How have I changed? It's hard to say. I get up earlier and don't worry about the little things. I don't take myself as seriously as I did a few years ago. I know what's most important in my life. And I cook breakfast almost every morning now! It's something I started when Brenda first came home from the hospital. I laugh out loud when I see my 8-year-old sitting at the kitchen table, eating his eggs and grits with the smoke alarm ringing loudly above him. He calmly tells his mom, "Oh, it's just Dad; he's burned the bacon again." I don't burn bacon any longer, and I can make some mean pancakes. Brenda even enjoys them.

# Breakfast with Brenda

"Breakfast with Brenda" was supposed to be a quaint little gathering of people in Birmingham who wanted to hear Brenda's story. She had told parts of it during newscasts and in her cancer series, and she had become known in the community as a strong, positive breast cancer survivor. The event was to be a supportive gathering for the breast cancer community, and to educate people about breast health. It turned out to be much bigger than expected, after the event organizers from ABC 33/40 and St. Vincent's Hospital were barraged by phone calls from people who wanted to attend.

The ballroom at the Wynfrey Hotel in Birmingham was filled with several hundred people when I walked to the podium to introduce my BW. She had asked me several times what I was going to say. Honestly, I wasn't sure. But the night before, I started getting that tingling feeling I get, and the words just started to flow.

*Whenever I make a speech before a local group, someone always comes up to mingle and make small talk. We exchange pleasantries, and then as we're shaking hands, they always say, "Thank you, Mr. Ladun, for coming." I'm known as Mr. Ladun to many people in the Birmingham area, and that's okay. As I always say, it all goes in the same bank account.*

*As a sports announcer, I meet heroes all the time—men and women who hit the winning shot, score the winning touchdown, or make the game-saving tackle. Today, I will introduce my hero. A hero is someone who meets her greatest fear head-on. My wife has gone head-to-head with one of the most despicable opponents of all time, cancer, and is winning the battle.*

*I fell in love with Brenda the first time I saw her stroll into the newsroom in Gainesville, Florida. She is completely captivating, vivacious, and spirited...a warm, strong, kind lady. She is not the kind of person to dissipate her energy in a display of bad temper or self-pity. In crucial situations, she gets a look in her eyes of inflexible determination. It means she has decided to do something and she will move heaven and earth to get it done.*

*She can charm the birds out of the trees, but what makes her exceptional is her strength of will. When she gets that look in her eyes, you can no more stop her than you can stop a runaway train on a downhill gradient. She is an irrepressible optimist with great inner confidence and strength. She has an indomitable fighting spirit. She has immaculate good manners and maturity beyond her years. She is the center of my universe. As I have often said, in a world of counterfeits, she is the genuine article. When Brenda enters a room, she's in Technicolor, and everyone else is in black and white.*

It was a defining moment.

# About the Author

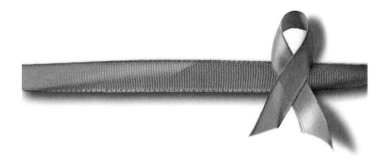

"The funny thing to me about having cancer," says Brenda Ladun, "was that it led to me getting awards." Since Brenda decided to go public with her struggle with breast cancer, she has received three significant awards in honor of her breast cancer awareness work.

• The Susan G. Komen Breast Cancer Foundation gave Brenda its Local Television Media Award for her extensive work toward raising awareness of breast cancer. This national award recognizes special relationships between Komen affiliates and local media partners. Brenda accepted on behalf of the Birmingham, Alabama, Komen affiliate. Brenda and ABC-33/40, through the news special "Cancer: A New Horizon" and their ongoing coverage of breast cancer issues, have advanced the Komen mission of eradicating breast cancer as a life-threatening disease.

• The American Cancer Society gave Brenda its Life Inspiration Award for her continuing efforts to educate the public about breast cancer.

• Brenda won a prestigious Edward R. Murrow Award for Radio and Television Journalism for her news series, "Cancer: A New Horizon."

People who turn to Brenda every night for news were not surprised when she was recognized nationally. She has worked in Birmingham television for fourteen years, and she's a five-time winner of Alabama Associated Press Awards for best investigative reporter and best specialized reporter. Most recently, Brenda won the Associated Press Award for best anchor. Brenda has also won several community awards for her work with the underprivileged. She works with the Grace House Christian Home for Girls, the Susan G. Komen Breast Cancer Foundation, as well as other community organizations.

Brenda communicates off-screen, too. Since going public with her cancer diagnosis, Brenda has spoken to church groups, civic groups, and at breast cancer events, always encouraging awareness and always encouraging people toward faith in God. Her "Breakfast with Brenda" event drew together hundreds of participants, many of them fighting breast cancer, many of them wearing telltale stylish hats. The sense of community was evident in the room.

But perhaps the best testimonies to Brenda's ministry come from the mouths of women who've had one-on-one contact with her, received a note or a phone call from her at a friend's request, or come up to her after she's spoken to a group. In Birmingham, Brenda Ladun has become known as someone willing to offer solace to those affected by breast cancer, to share meaningful Scriptures and pray together, to educate women about breast health, or just to listen and understand.

"To feel that close to a total stranger is incredible," Brenda says. "I can't explain the bond between cancer patients, but it's there. It's this incredible warm, loving feeling. We've all walked on the same path."